"The brain is faster than the mouth and the pen; but the heart is faster than the brain; and the mouth and pen take most of their orders from the heart."

from "The Autobiography of Nobody"

ISBN-13: [978-0615840833]
ISBN-10: [0615840833]

10 9 8 7 6 5 4 3 2 1
FIRST EDITION, July 2013
by Point Nine Publishing

ALSO BY AARON SAYLOR:
Sewerville: A Southern Gangster Novel

VISIT KEVIN HALL:
strother.wordpress.com

SEE MORE WORK BY ERICA CHAMBERS:
ericachambers.com

Kevin says...

I would like to thank my family and friends for their continued support and reality checks (and in some cases, actual checks, though cash is preferred). There are, of course, too many people to name individually, especially given the risk of leaving anyone out, but there are a few friends who deserve special love and attention for their love and attention.

Aaron (for encouraging this project in the first place);

Cory (for proof-reading and helping make sure jokes worked; if they don't, blame him);

Brandi (for being the first person to tell me "You should write a book" and for actually meaning it);

All the people who inspired the stories or whose memories I share in the essays (especially her, but then again, it's always about all the hers, really);

Jeff (who didn't do anything to help this project per se, but whose brotherhood is always present).

And to Norman. I wish you could have seen this.

Word.

Aaron says...

It's about time, Kevin.

Thanks everybody who got me this far: Mom, Dad, Mike, Sis, Brinton, Anthony, Cory, David, Daylan, Daxon, Chris, Nathan J., Sue, Pat, Karen, Kathryn, Jessica, Amy, Nan, KC & Donna, Kevin B., Berlin & Alma Sumner, Isaac Saylor, Betty Banks, Jimmy, Michelle, Gina, Dwight, Jimmy, Bobby, Marcus, Jerry, Tonya, Steven Goldmann, Alan Brewer, Thom Oliphant, Susan Bowman, Jason A., Zach, Matt, Greg, Cody M., Alison, Kay & Larry Epperson, Jim Johnson, Allen Willis, Stan Lee, Jack Kirby, John Romita, Steven Spielberg, George Lucas, *Fangoria* magazine, R.E.M., Roger Ebert, Chris Claremont, John Byrne, David Fincher, Ridley Scott, John Carpenter, Steve Earle, Neal Adams, Stephen King,

H.P. Lovecraft, Tom Petty, Isaac Asimov, Philip K. Dick, Quentin Tarantino, Don DeLillo, Harlan Ellison, Quiet Riot (RIP Kevin DuBrow), Twisted Sister, Bobby and Mary Coffey & The Movie Place, Johnny Bench, *The Baseball Bunch*, Alfred Hitchcock, Cawood Ledford, George Orwell, Edgar Allan Poe, Roger Corman, Martin Scorsese, Brian DePalma, Tom Cruise, Harold Campbell, Austin Wickline, Clint Eastwood, Tony Scott, John Buscema, Sam Raimi, Jack Buck, Tom Savini, Stan Winston, Wes Craven, Harry Chapin, Bruce Springsteen, Diane Davis, Bob Dylan, Mavis Townsend, Sherry Profitt, Eddie Murphy, Arnold Schwarzenegger, Sylvester Stallone, Girl Talk, Betty Craft, Michael Stone, Marty Brennaman, Joe Nuxhall, Pete Rose, Eric Davis, Barry Larkin, Kirk Gibson, Hal Jordan, Clark Kent, Bruce Wayne, Ted Turner, Bill Gates, Steve Jobs, Chuck Culpepper, John Milius, Video Solution in Stanton, Brown's IGA, faculty and staff of Powell County High School, Tom Marksbury, Anna Froula, Jerome Meckier, Lou Piniella, Harry Caray, Jr., Larry Hama, Jack Buck, Ron Bennington, Ron Diaz, Alex Trebek, Joe Stevenson, J.J. Abrams, John Candy, Dr. Charles Noss, Joyce Smallwood, the Stanton City basketball courts, Fred Rogers, Ryan Adams, Pete Yorn, *Sesame Street, 3-2-1 Contact,* Burt Reynolds, Oliver Stone, PT Anderson, Todd Snider, Evan Dando, Mike Myers, Robert DeNiro, Scotty Nguyen, Harold Ramis.

And more than anyone, Leslie Kay.

TABLE OF CONTENTS:

Introduction   11

The Autobiography of Nobody   19
Dear Charlie (An Open Letter to My Friend's
        Newborn Son)   35
FML Does Not Make Me LOL   41
The Dead on Black River   43
Is Being Good All It's Cracked Up to Be?   56
Forever Young   59
The Day I Fully Embraced My Age While
        Simultaneously Sticking It to the AARP   63
This is Why We Don't Take Family Vacations   69
Hold on to True Love Whenever You're Lucky Enough to
        Find It   73
Grandfathers   75
Sewerville: The Lay of the Land   77
Nonsense   85
Analyze This: A Promise Can Be A Pain in the Ass   105
The Sweet Smell of Pine Needles   107
The Price You Pay   117
Live Nude Girls (or, How 6-Year Old Kevin Remained
        Totally Confused About Movies and Life)   119
A Dark Room   123
Were You Raised in a Barnes (and Noble)? B&N Gets
        an "F" for Customer Service   127
Meet Me at the Monkey Bars   137
One Wreck to Rule Them All   139
Apep, the Darkness   143
Philosopher Dog (issue one)   157

About the Authors   193

INTRODUCTION

(this film has been modified from its original version. It has been formatted to fit your screen.)

Aaron: OK - give me one sec. I didn't see this window for some reason until now.

Kevin: OK.

Aaron: I was showing Leslie the called 3rd strike that ended last night's Rangers-Rays game.

Kevin: ha ha ha

Aaron: That was hilariously bad.

Kevin: Birddog Willoughby would not have approved of that call.

Aaron: No, he definitely would not have approved. They were showing some classics on ESPN tonight. One where a guy got stopped short sliding two feet from home plate, was tagged out, then the umpire called him a safe and he jumped up and stomped on home plate, laughing.

Kevin: oh, baseball.

Aaron: ok let's do this.

Kevin: So what do you have in mind?

Aaron: Basically just ask each other questions and jackass around with it. Like, I'll say, let's talk about this book, *Lost Change and Loose Cousins*. The title was a tag team effort, but you came up with the initial idea. Where did that come from?

Kevin: I've always liked the concept of musical collections of B-sides and rarities named things like "Orphans" or "Lost Dogs." At the time you first floated the idea of the project, I'd recently listened to an unreleased Springsteen track called "Loose Change," and the idea wouldn't leave me, but I thought it needed something else to balance it out. Given the small-town feel some of the stories, the family idea of "Cousins," seemed good. Plus, I'll use alliteration whenever possible. By the time you threw it back to me as *Lost Change and Loose Cousins*, I didn't even notice the switch until you pointed it out, asking if I'd seen the joke. The more I looked at it and said it out loud, the more I realized, "This is the title."

(Kevin strokes his chin, like a wise Chinese man in a shop full of mogwai.)

Kevin: You'd mentioned early on how this was something you wanted to do to keep the momentum going after *Sewerville* but before the next novel gets finished. What was the push there?

Aaron: Well, I believe in honesty so I'll start by saying that a small part of it was that I wanted to get some more work out there. I was away from writing for a few years and just felt my game rounding back into form. I was so happy with the way *Sewerville* turned out, wanting to get right back at it. I'd published a couple of short stories for download on-line, and some folks had mentioned to me that they wanted to see them in print because it was just easier for them to access. Not everyone has succumbed to the e-book revolution, and even for me there's just something better about having a good book in your hands. The look of it, the smell of it.

But more than that - and still being honest -- I'd been trying to get you to write something with me for a long time. For whatever reason we'd never gotten together on a project and I always thought it seemed like a good idea, working together like that - mostly because you're a good writer, but also partly because sometimes I need motivation and a writing partner seems like a good, constant kick in the ass.

Kevin: And, keeping in the theme of honesty, your success with *Sewerville* provided a kick here, both in terms of pure jealousy ("Hey, he has a book published!") and motivation ("Maybe I should actually try this, too").

Aaron: I guess it takes a little of everything. And here we are. I just assumed we would write a novel together but the more I thought about it, the more it seemed like a good chance to collect some things we've both built up over the last few years.

Kevin: My reluctance has mostly been from a fear of rejection -- I want people to like what I write, so that's been a bit of a delay until I could get past that and realize I'm not writing for anyone other than myself. Our last collaboration came when we were 19 and 20, and youthful arrogance made us too young to care if people liked it, mainly because we knew everyone should. Now, in our late 30s, well, I still want everyone to like it, but it's not the end of the world if they don't.

Aaron: You're not supposed to say "late 30's." It hurts my self-image.

Kevin: The grey hair in my beard is hard to argue against, though. Wait — we don't have author's photos, do we? What I meant was, for two insanely handsome 20-somethings...

(Nobody laughs.)

Let's talk about influences. Stephen King. You were the first person I've known who read him. For as long as I've known you (since sixth grade), you've been a fan of *Fangoria* magazine. Would sixth-grade Aaron be impressed with what current-day Aaron has written?

Aaron: I don't know. I hope so. As far back as I can remember - I'm talking before kindergarten - I've been a fan of science fiction, fantasy, and horror. It started with *Star Wars*, but before long I really loved horror more than anything. I mean, I read *Pet Sematary* in fourth grade, and I'd read a lot of short horror before that, and it just took hold. I'd say there are a few thousand writers our age that grew up with Stephen King and tried to emulate him at one time or another.

I've really made an effort in the last few years to write what I've always loved. *Sewerville*, I love that, too, but it's a different kind of love. I still flip through that book and think, okay, that was way better than I ever expected. But, it's a real-world story and right now, I really want to play in made-up worlds. Sixth-grade Aaron would not have cared very much about *Sewerville*, but he would have liked "The Dead on Black River" and he absolutely would have shit himself with excitement over the novel I'm working on right now, which is called *Ripsnorter* at the moment and is full-on horror. And I still love comic books as much as anything — my favorite piece in this book might be *Philosopher Dog*, which is a script I wrote that was intended to be the first issue in a short comic series. Maybe that one will live again. I hope so. [It's only in the paperback edition of *Lost Change and Loose Cousins* – Ed.]

Kevin: That title - *Ripsnorter* - is as "Aaron" of a title as anything I've heard. It just sounds exactly like something you would have shown me in *Fangoria* when we sat in Mr. Abner's classroom.

Aaron: Really? I have a feeling the title will change by the time I'm done.

Kevin: Anyone who has read *Sewerville* would argue it's full-on horror, in its own way...

Aaron: I can see that. Meth and pills, they really turn people into monsters, inside and out. It's fitting what you say about the title *Ripsnorter*

— that it reminds you of something from *Fangoria* back in the 1980s -- since I want it to be a throwback. I guess when you get to be our age, you spend a lot of time thinking about your past.

Kevin: That's very true. Most of what I've contributed has been a look back at childhood memories from an adult's perspective. This is true for the essays and the fictional pieces; I don't think I've ever written a fictional story that wasn't presented as something filtered through the narrator's memory. Perhaps that's a goal for Aaron/Kevin's Book Two.

But take something like "One Wreck to Rule Them All," which was a huge impact on me as a child. I went at least a year telling people I'd never want to have my own license; I was simply afraid of cars. I never really took the time to (and I almost hate using this word because it's so touchy-feely, but it's the only one to use) *process* what happened. It's a story I'd wanted to write for a long time, in large part because I thought it had one of the strongest first sentences I'd ever written, but I'd never actually worked through the wreck itself. When I sat down to write, I was back there on that road, watching it all happen again. It led to some great discussions with my mom about that day.

Aaron: It's interesting. Whenever I read something I wonder how much of the work is the author just re-telling his own story. Some of what you've put in *Lost Change and Loose Cousins* is obviously one hundred percent nonfiction, but the stories like "Nonsense," I wasn't sure.

Kevin: That's always the one people ask about -- "Is that true?" Or they start to ask then back off, probably because they think they want to know but are afraid to be certain. That said, it's fiction. Mostly.

Aaron: Good.

Kevin: I'd also like to point out that "Meet Me at the Monkey Bars" is 100 percent fiction. I never sent anyone that letter. I just thought it would be fun to show a socially awkward person get more and more disturbing as he kept writing. Most people say they can get their thoughts down better on paper, and this particular narrator just couldn't do that. Or maybe he did and said exactly what he wanted and has no clue it was inappropriate.

Aaron: I thought it was about Laura Dennis.

Kevin: If you'd gone to Stanton Elementary, you'd know that the only girl for me in kindergarten was Martina Crabtree.

Aaron: I did go to Stanton Elementary.

Kevin: I thought you went to Bowen. And this, ladies and gentleman, is how we learn that even in the nonfiction, we have what's called an unreliable narrator.

Aaron: I moved to Bowen Elementary halfway through 2nd grade. I was in Ms. Arnett's kindergarten class. With Martina. I'm just saying.

Kevin: We've both been influenced quite a bit, it seems, from our days in Powell County [Kentucky – *Ed*.]. It was a fictionalized setting for *Sewerville*. Do you plan on it being a home for more of your stories, even the ones that have more of a supernatural approach?

Aaron: I think so. It seems natural to do it that way because it *has* been such a big influence, for better or worse. I realized about halfway through writing *Sewerville* that the real subtext of that book is that it's about me leaving our hometown and not wanting to go back there. Back there to live, I mean. I just couldn't do it – I like Thai food, Indian food, Best Buy, the mall, and I can't get that in Powell County. Incidentally, Sewardville, KY first makes an appearance in an old story I wrote, "Somewhere Between Heaven and Hell,"[Not included in this book. – *Ed*.] and is also referenced in "Apep, the Darkness."

Kevin: I'm sure other authors have done it, but that repeated use of a central town is another of King's influences.

Aaron: Maybe, but like you say, it's a fairly common device. Still I won't deny that I am aware of Castle Rock, Maine.

Kevin: The characters often get drawn from people we knew, or at least knew of. The stories and characters from Powell County are almost too unreal to be real. I think it was David Rogers that once said something along the lines of how a great TV show could be made about Powell County except that *Twin Peaks* already exists. What other writers would you say have been your biggest influences?

Aaron: Philip K. Dick. Faulkner. Don DeLillo. A book by Tim O'Brien called *In the Lake of the Woods*. It's hard to say. There have been so many. I've been influenced by Steven Spielberg and Martin Scorsese maybe as much as anything, when it comes to storytelling.

Kevin: For me, the earliest influence was from the late David Rule, former pastor at the church I attended as a child. He often started a sermon with a thought, preached on about other things, then tied it all back together with a bow at the end. I straight up copied that when I got older. On a national level, I would pay people sums of money to say "You clearly read Rick Bragg," because I think he's the best pure story-teller I've ever heard and read. He has a way with Southern language that makes you crave sweet tea while swatting away mosquitoes. And, as odd as it sounds, I've had people say some of the stuff is like Michael Ian Black, which I think is high praise. He's a funny fella. Having said that, I think it might be about time to let the readers decide for themselves.

Aaron: Where do you have to be? What are you, trying to get laid?

Kevin: Isn't that the goal for anybody who picks up a guitar, paintbrush, pen, whatever? Awards are nice, but give us money and women. (And fade to black.)

LOST
CHANGE
AND
LOOSE
COUSINS

POINT NINE PUBLISHING

THE AUTOBIOGRAPHY OF NOBODY

By Aaron Saylor

1

I am seven years old. Brinton is seven years old. We are seven years old.

The summer sun shimmers above us two little boys, as we whack through the briar thicket with our tobacco stick swords. The sticks are faded gray, pointed on one end. Tall as a seven-year old boy, taller than a seven-year old boy. Our game is Greek Gods, and we gods are on a mission to find Athena in the jungles of mortal Earth.

Whenever we play this game, Brinton is always Zeus, and I am always Apollo. We never argue about it. He assumes the role of Zeus, god of gods, just like he wants, and I assume the role of Apollo, god of the sun and the arts, just like I want. This is perfectly acceptable to our seven-year old brains: perfect roles for perfect little boys, perfect little boys playing under a perfect sun on a perfect day in what must be the only perfect corner of the universe.

I wield my weapon. Briars fall. Mosquitoes nip at my sunburned neck. I am not thinking about grown-up things; I don't care about girls or taxes or law school or divorce or alcoholism or colonoscopies. These issues lie far down the road, deep in the underbrush, much too far away for a little boy of seven to know or care anything about.

Now, I don't know or care about anything except playing Greek Gods with my best friend, in the summer between first and second grades. I think only little-boy things, fun things, pretty things, immediate things, things that are not Coming, things that are only Now.

The wooden tobacco-stick sword in my hand. The sun in my face. The briars knifing my skinny legs. Blood on my elbow. My little brother. Granny and Mom, back at the house. Dinner. And my best friend, five steps ahead of me. My best friend, five steps ahead of me. My best friend… my best friend… my best friend…

We keep the past alive because it keeps us alive.

＊

I'm thirty-one now. Somewhere along the way I learned a nasty secret: little boys do not grow up to become Greek Gods. I could have done without knowing that.

＊

Something else I learned along the way: people haven't yet gotten a handle on time.

So often we treat time like a rocket ship – like we're hurtling forward on its back, into the Great Eternal Whatever, leaving infinite numbers of precious moments with no chance of ever revisiting them. A ride to tomorrow, but no ticket back to yesterday. You can't go back again, They say. No crying over spilled milk, They say. What's done is done, keep your head down and just worry about the things in front of you. That's what They say. That's what They want you to believe.

I disagree, though. I disagree with They a lot, you will come to understand that. I think that time is a window, and we can jump back and forth through that window whenever we want.

Look, I just jumped through, it's today.

Look, I just jumped back through to the other side, it's last week.

Look, now it's today again.

Now, a month ago.

No wait, I'm seven now.

Now it's last February.

Now it's yesterday, I was in tenth grade.

Now it's today again.

Then it's the first time we met, don't you remember? And it's today. And it's yesterday. And you were so beautiful; then we got married; the kids started school; you were so beautiful; I was a jackass; you were so beautiful; God, you are still so beautiful.

It's today, yesterday, today, tomorrow, all at once but also, somehow, never at the same time.

Back and forth, just like that, people move through time, in word and thought and hope and dream. Our hearts seek shelter through whatever window offers the safest view. Flying in rocket ships, jumping through windows, looking for shelter — pick your metaphor.

This remains: we live in the past as much as we live in the present as much as we live in the future. So, here then is another metaphor, and a much better one, for the purposes of what I am trying to tell you with this Autobiography of Nobody. Which is this: life moves not on a line, but in a flash. In a series of flashes. And these flashes, they pop and fade against consciousness, sometimes bright to the fore and sometimes dim in the background. But no matter what — NO MATTER WHAT — the flashes never disappear completely. They remain for whenever the heart requires, and the flashes that the heart requires most, burn brightest and closest.

If I ask, where did you sit at your mother's funeral? you can tell me. *I sat on the left side of the chapel, front and center, next to Dad.* This is a dim flash, though, less shelter for your heart, and so it quickly burns and then moves back into the dusky corners of your memory.

Try it again. If I ask you, what did she look like the moment you asked her to marry you? another flash explodes. *She smiled. Perfect white tears shone in her green eyes, hovered on her lashes, fell quietly down her cheeks and into my hand.* Yes. This flash is bright. It stays longer. And it didn't have far to go to get to the front, either. Your heart keeps it ready when needed.

That's the idea. We keep the past alive because it keeps us alive.

*

What the hell am I talking about? I never had a wife.

2

I get drunk sometimes. It's only fair that I bring this up now. On top of getting drunk, I take medicine, too. Well, I don't just take it. They give it to me. They give me a lot of medicine, actually quite a lot, red pills and blue bills and plastic-coated yellow pills, with names I can't pronounce, not that you would recognize those names, anyway.

Sometimes, my medicine ends up getting mixed with things with which it is not meant to be mixed. But only sometimes, and certainly not enough of the time for me to be considered anything like dangerous, or addicted, or even an alcoholic. But, to be fair about this: some times, sometimes happens more often than it happens other times. Some times, sometimes helps me feel better. You know.

Oh — I also need to tell you one other thing. When I get on my medicine, my mind wanders off track and it can be hard for people outside my head to keep up. Just bringing that up before it gets a little out of hand. Don't worry: I will try to keep it sensible enough so as not to irritate you too badly. But still. You know. I know you know. Thanks.

3

Thoughts scatter sometimes, between the brain and the hand. They make good sense while formulated as neural energy – a smooth narrative, easily understood in the thinking, but lost in communication. The brain is faster than the mouth and the pen; but the heart is faster than the brain; and the mouth and pen take most of their orders from the heart.

It probably would be best if I started my story with the parts which you will all find most believable. This is not to say that some of my story is *not* to be believed; my autobiography is, make no mistake about it, a completely reliable record of my life to this point. I do, however, wish to present this record in as agreeable a manner as might be possible, and not insult the reader with false claims of fact.

I do not intend to offend my audience's intelligence or have doubt cast upon either me or those with whom I have crossed paths during the course of my many days and nights in this world. Certainly, I am acutely aware that asking a reader to entertain as truth events that appear outlandish and fantastical would be to strike a harsh blow against my credibility. I also am acutely aware that in the telling of one's own story, one's credibility is of paramount importance.

And so, with both of the aforementioned thoughts in mind, I preface the rest of my story with this comment: some things in this world are believable, and some things are simply to be believed, and very often, that which is believable and that which is to be believed are entirely separate things —independent of each other.

In the pages that follow, there are incidents described in ways that would seem to strain the very limits of believability. I recognize that. Ghosts are difficult for some to accept; though specters do reside in our world, they seem content to hide in the corners of our eye, to breathe their chill breath just over our shoulders, to stay just far enough out of sight to allow the question as to their existence. Demons, too. Much the same — all teeth and horns and hairy chests and cloven hoofs — who could believe that? And who could believe in living shadows? Or angels? Even beautiful angels? And monsters — all sorts of monsters, in the closet, under the bed, in the woods behind the house, in the hallways at school.

These are all among the sorts of characters which have crossed my path at one time or another and which I emphatically understand have been disavowed as fantasy by most everyone who considers themselves sane. And yet, much as these creatures do seem unbelievable to level minds, level minds should believe in them no less. As unreal as you might find ghosts and demons and angels and living shadows and all sorts of monsters, I can only assure you that they *are* real. As real as the face in the mirror.

But as I said, ghosts and angels and demons and monsters and banshees and Pentecostal-preaching carnival barkers come later. Pike and the dead monkeys come later. Joey Wadcutter comes later. It all comes later, it all comes later, it all comes later, but rest assured, when later it does all come, it will all be real. *Real.* I am pretty good at telling stories. I am not nearly as good at making them up.

4

Now, the easy parts.

One day, I was born. Believe that. Also believe that I would prefer to say that I sprang fully-formed from the head of my father, but, sadly, such is not the case. Instead, my first rendezvous with the mortal coil happened in a hospital delivery room — no doubt a room similar to the one where you were born. There was a doctor, a nurse or two, my mom and dad, some blood, some amniotic fluid. The tile on the floor of the room was bright green and sterile, save for a few choice body liquids. There was some grunting, some screaming, then I popped out and there was a lot of crying. I, Mom, and Dad — we all cried a lot. Dad's nerves got the best of him and he ran into the hallway and threw up. My mother held me for a moment, just before the nurse whisked me away to be weighed, cleaned, and prepared for the rest of my life. Then my mother and I spent a day or two in her hospital room together, with my father sleeping when he could in an armchair by the window. They named me James Aaron Saylor, James after my maternal grandfather, Aaron because they liked the sound of it, Saylor because it was their last name and also because they figured it would keep the family name alive, me being the first-born son and all.

After that, the immediate details remain fuzzy, but the general idea is that my birth was not much different than millions of other births around the world.

*

Now, some quick notes about the people who first made me. Most of this will come up again later and in more detail, so no need to memorize.

Dad.

My father got all the athletic genes in his side of the family, but you wouldn't know it by looking at him. In terms of physique, Richard Isaac Saylor is nothing special. Point of fact, he's a short man — 5' 5" on his tallest day. Dad battles gout on a regular basis, and suffers from a spastic colon, too.

Yet despite his lack of physical stature, Dad is a man of superhuman athletic ability. Amazing, how quick and graceful he could move when called into action. I have played a lot of sports against a lot of people, winning some and losing others, but never have I endured an athletic defeat so merciless as those I received at the hands of my father.

Here is a Simple Fact of Life: my father is the best golfer, tennis player, bowler, baseball thrower, horseshoe tosser, rock climber, fish catcher, game hunter, sport shooter, car racer, and basketball player I have ever known.

It goes almost without saying that in our all-time history of father-son games, the running score is right now: DAD — 14,562 victories. SON — 0 victories. Zero. I kept track all these years and I can tell you for certain that I have never beaten my Dad at anything. Not even a footrace. Not even a video game. Not even all the times when he tried to let me win. While I would love to tell you that nowadays *I* try to let *him* win just to keep his sense of pride healthy because of course there is no way that a man in his mid-fifties can compete with a healthy younger man in his athletic prime (such as I am), the truth is, Dad wins all the time because he just plain ol' beats my ass.

If I were the head of marketing for a gigantic shoe company — Nike, Reebok, Adidas, name one — I would immediately sign my Dad to a multi-million dollar endorsement deal. Imagine the creative and humorous potential for an athletic shoe ad campaign that would feature a fifty-five year old man with gout and a spastic colon!

Anyway, there are a lot of great things I could say about my Dad but right now it's enough to tell you that he is a superhero. The rest will come out soon enough.

Mom.

My mother was a genius. Was, and is. Unmitigated. Undeniable. Not a "freak of nature" kind of genius, not playing-Bach-concertos-backwards-and-one-handed-at-age-four kind of genius, but a genius nonetheless. I know that at one point her IQ was measured somewhere in the neighborhood of 210. My mother can learn anything and can teach you anything. Calculus, plumbing, computer programming, Euclidian geometry, anthropological theory, guitar, German. When she was a junior in high school she took a German language test, and scored higher on it than anybody else in the southeastern United States. (I am quite certain that she would have scored higher than anyone in the entire country if anyone in the entire country had been allowed to take the test against her.)

Example. We had a puzzle in the house. The kind where you jump pegs over each other, removing the ones you've jumped until at last there is only one peg left. Generally, this type of puzzle has around fifteen pegs, but my mom managed to get her hands on a version that had about fifty, maybe more. Round plastic pegs, stuck in a wooden cross. Since I was no good at the puzzle with fifteen pegs, you can imagine what type of a miserable failure I was at the one with fifty. I just couldn't do it, just plain could not solve the thing, no matter how hard I tried. But, of course, Mom could. She solved the puzzle on her first try — like it was nothing, like it was changing her shirt or brushing her teeth. And then, to teach me how to do it, she wrote a computer program that explained it all. With graphics. Just for the hell of it. Just because she could. That's my mother.

Growing up, Mom quickly discovered a love for books and movies, and she carried that love with her into adulthood. Still carries it to this day. Fortunately, she shared those loves with her children, and in doing so ensured that imagination ruled our house. In my earliest memory, I am three years old, lying in my mother's bed with my head on her shoulder, falling asleep while she whispers the Sesame Street version of "The Princess and the Pea," into my ear. The window is open, a summer wind kisses my eyelids and —

Tell you what. Let's stop there. More about Mom later.

*

Brother. Sister.

Oh, damn. Have to hold off on my brother and sister for right now. More about them later, too.

*

Mom and Dad divorced when I was five years old. At least, I think I was five. For the sake of honesty, I have to say that I'm not really sure of the exact date that It All Went Down. Let's see: my sister was born when I was three — I know Mom and Dad were married then — and I don't think they were married when I started kindergarten (five), but for certain they definitely were not married when I entered second grade, and noticed my mother marking herself "divorced" on the annual parental paperwork.

If you are in second grade, and you want to have fun some sweaty August afternoon, ask your mother what "divorced" means.

Anyway, whenever it happened, it happened, and that was that. Didn't much affect my routine. Dad was away at work most of the time up until then, so when the divorce hit it just seemed to me that he was away at work for increasingly long periods of time. A few days, a week, a month, whatever. La-dee-dah. It might seem strange, my being oblivious to what most people would consider such a pivotal life moment, but the truth is, I was a little boy and little boys don't care about anything but themselves. Beyond that, they certainly DO NOT care about a concept so bizarre and alien as marriage, much less the dissolution of a marriage. Little boys care about Batman and *Star Wars* and *The Dukes of Hazzard*, about Saturday morning cartoons, and new tennis shoes, and official Snoopy fishing poles, and getting a leather jacket like the one Fonzie wears on the old television show.

My parents knew that we children would not understand what was going on with them. For that reason, they saw no point in telling us. There was never an official divorce announcement to my siblings or me. Nobody ever sat us down to explain the intricacies of asset sharing, or child support, or visitation rights. Basically, they left it up to us to understand it on our own, and on our own terms, and that's exactly what we did. Slowly, we grew into the truth. At first there was the gradual realization that Dad was spending more and more nights away from home, missing more and more birthdays and ballgames. Then, a few days without seeing him became a week. One week became two. Two weeks became a month, a month became six months, six months became... well, six months became more than six months.

The longest I have ever gone without seeing my father is three years. That was the span between my high school graduation and my sister's. That's really more my fault than his.

Just hitting the main points here.

*

Okay, maybe this can't wait after all. I want to tell you a quick story about my brother. I was going to hold off but this thought just won't go away.

James Aaron Saylor and John Michael Saylor were born eighteen months apart, me in May of 1975 and him in October of '76. As I said earlier, I was named James Aaron after my grandfather and some guy who had a nice-sounding name. My brother, on the other hand, was named John Michael after my *mother's* grandfather (John) and some other guy with a nice-sounding name (Michael). So, you can see, we had something in common from the beginning.

My mom wanted a second son so that her children could have someone with whom to grow up, side by side. And grow up side by side, we did — inseparable from the moment we could walk and talk together, hide and seek, kickball in the yard, throw the whiffle ball around, play with the dogs, everything. A lot of older brothers get some sort of attitude about younger siblings, like they're too young to be worth anything except maybe as a punching bag or a target for BB guns. I never had that problem. I loved my brother, he was my best friend under the sun, and I did everything I could to protect him from this world. Then one day, when I was seven — well, practically seven, six years three months and eleven days to be precise – Michael and I were running through the woods, chasing each other with rotten tree limb swords in hand, and my brother fell into a deep hole in the ground and never came back out.

*

I am not good with plants. Or pets. I try, but can't quite figure out the trick to nurturing other living creatures. They usually die on me quicker than they seem to die on other people.

Normally, I throw the plants in the dumpster and bury the pets in my back yard, underneath the maple tree I planted when I first bought the house. But I lost my shovel in the second grizzly bear attack, so now I just throw everything out with the trash and let the garbage company do their thing. Thank goodness I don't have children.

＊

My mother's love of imagination took root in me and thrived. She read stories to us kids every night. Many of those nights, she read until we couldn't possibly keep our eyes open for one more second, which meant that the next night she would have to go back and re-read the same sections just so we wouldn't miss anything. Then there were other nights when we begged her to read until she could barely keep her own eyes open, and we begged her to keep reading and she read some more anyway. Sometimes we got two or more short stories – Brothers Grimm, Hans Christian Andersen, Aesop, Uncle Remus, Sesame Street, Dr. Seuss, the fundamental kids' stuff — and other times, we got a whole novel spread out over several nights – *Tom Sawyer, Huckleberry Finn, Treasure Island, King Arthur and His Knights of the Round Table.*

Then, as I got older, and could read to myself, I absorbed every book I could get my hands on. I didn't really have a favorite style or genre or author; *all* genres and *all* authors were my favorite. Nowadays, I prefer 18th and 19th century English gothic literature, but as a boy I cast my lot randomly and reveled in whatever I reeled in. Outer space, dragons, army, sharks, knights, Hardy Boys, gods, monsters, science, legend, *Boys' Life, Time, Newsweek, Psychology Today,* the newspaper, whatever, whatever. Anywhere I went, I went there with a book or magazine in my hands. I quickly became the "quiet kid," the kid who went to family reunions and birthday parties and disappeared into a room by himself, just to read.

It was a natural progression for me, going from reading other people's stories to thinking I could write my own. Actually, I wrote my first story in crayola, at age four — a one-pager about a snake in the woods. Before long, I cranked out my first collection of short stories (age 10, *Songs from the Treehouse*), a book of poetry (age 12, *Poems*), and two cookbooks (also at age 12, *Cooking with Aaron* and *In the Kitchen*). At 16 I self-published a novel called *Somewhere Between Heaven and Hell,* about a general in Satan's army that escapes from Hell to reunite with the soul of a lost love reincarnated in the body of a librarian in southeastern Ohio. I really like that story. In a short span of time that amazed even me, it ended up on the desk of an editor at Hyperion Publishing in New York, and twelve months after that *Somewhere Between Heaven and Hell* was in your local bookstore, where you no doubt saw it and became one of the 13 million people that put it on the *New York Times* bestseller list for 113 straight weeks, 31 consecutive at #1. A stunning achievement, you must admit.

What? You didn't read the book? Well, maybe you saw the movie. It hit multiplexes in the summer of 2002 (dropping the *Somewhere* from the title, which I never understood), starring Tom Cruise and directed by Steven Spielberg to the tune of $268 million box-office dollars and four Oscar nominations. No wins, though. Dammit. Life sucks. Then, again, I wasn't nominated for anything because the film's producers more or less froze me out of the production process, which is par for the course when it comes to authors and Hollywood, so I'm kind of glad it didn't win anything. I took the money and ran, to flog the appropriate verbal dead horse.

You never knew.

Most people didn't.

Of course, the majority of that little story is fiction.

I did write a story when I was four about a snake in the woods, but the rest of my literary career was fabricated just now. The brain is faster than the mouth and the pen; but the heart is faster than the brain; and the mouth and the pen take most of their orders from the heart.

In reality, my writing career derailed — famous and fortunate though it was destined to become — when I watched *Raiders of the Lost* Ark and decided that the movies would be my new mistress. Don't know why that happened, can't explain why, won't even try to explain why. I was six years old, it happened, that's that.

From that point on, I immersed myself in movies the way I immersed myself in books all the years before. I went to our town's drive-in theater practically every weekend during the summer, two movies on the front screen Friday, two more on the back screen Saturday. During the week, I wore out the carpet at every movie rental store in town, one or two movies a night during school months and four or five a day during the summer. I would name some of the stuff I watched during these formative years, but it would take forever and probably not add much to the conversation.

My tastes in movies were as varied as my tastes in literature. I loved a bloody slasher flick as much as I loved a historical costume drama with French subtitles. Safe to say, if you can think of a movie title that was released theatrically or direct-to-video between 1985 and 2000, chances are, I have seen it. At the very least, I picked up the case in a video store somewhere and *thought* about seeing it.

Seeing all those movies was more than enough to convince me that there was plenty of room in this world for a man who wanted to create a quality film. After all, so many of the movies I saw were complete and utter shit. I figured: what the hell, if somebody can release crap like that for the viewing public to suffer through, then surely I can actually come up with something *good* and really blow the doors off. So, I bought a few books on the trade, and soon enough taught myself how to be a screenwriter.

5

I could have been valedictorian of my high school class if I really wanted to, but I didn't, so I wasn't. This is a corollary proof of my theory that a man can achieve any goal on which he sets his sights, if not for liquor.

*

Quit college after my first year, moved to Los Angeles in the summer of 1994. I vowed to my mother that if I didn't sell a screenplay before I turned twenty-five years of age, I would give up the pipe dream, go back to school, and live a "normal" life.

Now, in my mind, there was absolutely no way that I would ever fail in my endeavor. It was simple math. I read in one of my screenwriting books that ten thousand or so scripts are submitted to movie production companies each year. I have no proof that number is accurate, but hey – it worked for me at the time. Eighty percent of those submitted scripts are immediately tossed in the garbage because the writer fails to follow a series of simple format rules: brass brads (those little thumb-tack-looking things that go through the holes on the left side of the paper), no crazy spiral binding, simple courier font, no overly prettified title page, crap like that. Check. Not a problem with me. I learned the basics inside out, and immediately, I made the cut into the top 20%.

Next, an additional 15% of the ten thousand are dumped because the idea is not movie-worthy – one hundred and twenty pages of a computer geek talking to the guy in the next cubicle. One hundred pages of a receiving clerk's daily routine. Ninety-five pages of yoga mysticism. So forth. When it came to this, I was not worried about my ideas.

So, out of ten thousand scripts, 95% hit the circular file immediately. That leaves about five hundred, and my trusty handbook told me that of those remaining five hundred, only about a hundred approach feasibility and the rest succumb to some storytelling malady or another — structure problems, second-act issues, slow movement, weak character arcs. That leaves one hundred or so new scripts a year out of ten thousand which get serious attention and can actually put a struggling young writer on the map. Folks, if you've been keeping up with the math, you know that equates to a whopping 1%. A writer needs to be in the top 1% of all submitted scripts to have any shot.

Of course, I was pretty confident I could do that. I like to think I'm in the 1%.

But, there's something my little handbook didn't tell me, which I found out when I actually started knocking on doors in the movie business. The fact is, those ten thousand scripts don't really mean shit. Most studios and production companies don't even look at outside work; they take a pitched idea – usually from a star or a director – and then commission their own scripts and go from there.

God, the movie business sucks.

Still, I had my goal – a sale by the age of twenty-five. And praise all fates, I got a sale at twenty-two. Then another. And another.

I ended up back in school anyway.

We will return to this. But I told you – these are the easy parts. I am hitting the main points here.

*

God?
Destiny?

Love?
Life?
Mysteries?
Questions?
Answers?
Answers!
I get headaches.

*

I believe in love. I know love is real, not just a product of Hollywood marketing departments and bad romance novelists. I have even been in love myself a few times. I'm not in love right now, though. The last girlfriend I had left me for a guy who worked in a detox center and cleaned puke out of urinals for a living.

*

I'm not sure who They is, but They definitely have seen a lot of the world, don't you think?

Life, as They say, is just one long series of turning points — a left here, a right there, away from home, back again, away and back, away and back. Pull up to the stoplight, cut the wheel, punch the gas, go, hope you don't hit the idiot coming from the other direction. There is a lot to remember when you pull up to that stoplight, but one of the most important is this: you are always the idiot coming from the other direction.

I wouldn't stay long in L.A., just long enough to figure out that maybe I wasn't cut out for the entertainment world, after all. So many meetings with HOLLYWOOD AGENTS and PRODUCTION COMPANY EXECS, so little to show for it. A couple of option agreements, a music video, a commercial or two — written by "anonymous," as far as the general public was concerned — and nothing much else. I felt sick; I had looked behind the curtain, saw the Wizard in his shiny hat and shiny coat, then realized he was just another jackass with trendy hair and a bad coke habit. Imagine, a fat old man with a cocaine habit, at the dawn of the 21st century. Sad. Cocaine was such a 1980's thing.

*

Those are the easy parts.

Bring me a glass of wine. And my medicine — it's time for my medicine. I know I'm not supposed to mix them but sometimes I do, we've already been over that already. Has anybody seen my brother? Let's go back to that now. It's important. Maybe if I can tell you that story now, this will all start to make sense.

Remember, always remember: Thoughts scatter sometimes, between the brain and the hand. The brain is faster than the mouth and the pen; but the heart is faster than the brain; and the mouth and pen take most of their orders from the heart. At least that's how it works with me, anyway.

DEAR CHARLIE (AN OPEN LETTER TO MY FRIEND'S NEWBORN SON)

by Kevin Hall

Dear Charlie,

Let me tell you about Wilco.

First, though, let me make a few introductions: my name is Kevin. You're going to get to know me pretty well over the years, but for now, I'll hit the basics of what you should know: Springsteen. Wilco. Scorsese. Tarantino. Football. *Seinfeld. Arrested Development. The Simpsons.* Football. When you learn to talk, if you're remotely familiar with any of those things, we'll get along just fine.

You see that man over there? Probably not, because although I know little about babies who are about 12 hours old, I'm fairly certain I recall reading that they can't see long distances. OK, so how about this? The next time the bearded redhead holds you, the one in the Phillies cap, that's your dad. His name is Cory. I've known him a long time, and one thing I know about him more than just about anything else, he's waited for this day more than you (or anyone) can possibly imagine (realizing, of course, you are 12 hours old and can't imagine anything right now, but even when you are much much older, the sentiment will be the same).

Charlie, I first met your dad when he was 6 or 7 years old. He was precocious, which is a fancy way of saying "your dad was a bratty little turd." At that time, in the mid-1980s, he was rather well known in Powell County because he was, even at that young age, a regular columnist for *The Clay City Times.* The debate raged (still does to some) over how much writing your dad actually did for his column, but anyone who knows Cory knows full well that he still writes like a 6-year-old.

His "Cory's Comments" column proved to be a must-read for Powell Countians, and I was no exception. It seemed everyone who was anyone wanted to interact with your dad in hopes of getting a few sentences of fame in our small-town newspaper. One summer day, while at the farm of our county's agricultural agent, I finally had my chance for the spotlight, as I delighted your dad repeatedly by showing him how a dog could sit and shake hands. As he laughed, I envisioned my future glory, knowing that teachers and fellow students alike at Stanton Elementary would marvel at my dog-command skills, and for a week, I'd be the toast of the town, or at least the fifth grade.

When the newspaper finally published the next week, Charlie, you cannot fathom my surprise when I failed to warrant even the scantest mention in your dad's column. I no longer remember the content he chose over me, but suffice it to say it paled in comparison to my ability to shake hands with a dog.

Yes, Charlie, I'm still bitter.

But that's really not the point. I'm still getting there (another thing you'll no doubt learn about me: I can be long-winded, but I always have a point, and I will tie everything together in the end).

Now, Charlie, I take you back to late 1994 or early 1995 at Powell County High School. It was the night of a basketball game, and as I walked down the steps from the concession area upstairs, I passed by a young redheaded guy going up the stairs. At the time, my friend Aaron and I were planning our second season of an ill-fated radio show in Stanton, and I knew your dad was a fan. Seeing him on those stairs, I pounced on the chance to bring him into the fold and onto the show, pitching it as a way to do an updated "Cory's Comments" but over the airwaves instead of print. He accepted immediately.

To say that my life changed that day would be an understatement.

Charlie, I honestly can't imagine my life without your dad in it. We became fast friends, going almost everywhere together (except to a Weezer concert that I honestly thought was for ages 18-plus), and perhaps no night was his involvement more noticeable than a summer night in 1996. That's the night, Charlie, that your dad helped me meet the woman who would become my wife (OK, so she eventually became my ex-wife, but let's just ignore that for now).

Standing in front of Delta Gas in the middle of Stanton, my group of friends and I kept noticing two girls in a convertible driving around the circle. Nobody had the guts to motion for them to pull over, although I kept talking about wanting to do so. Finally, your dad had enough and called me a name that I can't print here but can explain it this way: you know that area you came out of a few hours ago when you entered this world? That's what he called me.

I accepted the challenge, flagged the girls down, rode around town with them, and the next thing you know, a few years later we were married. The marriage didn't last, Charlie, and that's a hard fact of life you'll learn: not every story comes out perfect in the end. Life is tough, but sometimes the friends who help you start the story will still be there when an unexpected end comes into play.

Your dad is that friend, Charlie.

But Charlie, I don't mean to make it sound like your dad is a saint. No parent is perfect, and in an odd way, that's really what makes them perfect, and if imperfection is the measuring point then your dad might be as perfect as it gets.

You see, Charlie, your dad and I haven't always gotten along. We've almost had fistfights more times than I can count. We've had shouting matches. We've said cruel, hateful things.

And once we went years without talking.

The reasons don't matter, other than to say we were both wrong, and we were both stubborn.

What matters, though, are two things: one, even despite being on non-speaking terms, your dad still came to my wedding, realizing that even though times might have been rough for us at that exact moment, perhaps the friendship was worth investing in just in case somewhere down the line we patched things up again.

Here's the other thing that matters: we patched things up again. One evening in the summer of 2002, I came home from work, checked my email and found a note called "olive branch." It was from your dad.

I don't recall the exact wording, but it was along the lines of how it was time to let bygones be bygones and if a once-powerful friendship could somehow find a way to heal, then he would be in favor of it.

Now, Charlie, here's why I want to tell you about Wilco. Your dad's words hit me hard, and I couldn't let them go unnoticed. I agreed to try to become friends again, and as part of my own olive branch offering, I invited him to see Wilco as they toured for *Yankee Hotel Foxtrot*.

That night at the Brown Theatre in Louisville, we sat in the second row and marveled at the music before us. In that moment, the past wasn't forgotten; it was just put aside as lessons learned.

Charlie, we haven't looked back.

Since then, your dad and I have become brothers which is what happens when you go through things, both good and bad, that can barely be put into words. Charlie, the day will come in which you'll find yourself hanging out with Lollapalooza VIPs playing kickball or recovering from tragedies so immense they still seem unreal, but either way, I hope you have someone like your dad by your side much like I did. He is my friend, my brother, the Little Steven to my Springsteen (I'm writing this, so I can full well allow myself to be Bruce in this scenario).

Charlie, this man who holds you will mess up. I assure you that he will. But more importantly, this man who holds you will give you everything he has, for as long as he can.

I tell you that with certainty because he's done that for me.

So, Charlie, today, in honor of you coming into this world, and for every Jan. 15 from here on out, I will listen to *Yankee Hotel Foxtrot*. I'm not sure I'd be writing to you today without that album, and for that, I'm forever grateful to Wilco.

Oh, and Charlie, when you wear that Wilco jumper I gave your parents at their baby shower, now you'll know what it really means. Yes, some people raised their eyebrows and wondered why one of Cory's closest friends didn't get a more elaborate gift, opting instead for something plugging one of my favorite bands.

The truth is, Charlie, that shirt, and the lyrics printed on it, represent the past, the present and the future. Your shirt says "Wilco loves you, baby."

Charlie, we all do.

FML DOES NOT MAKE ME LOL

by Kevin Hall

I hate chat-based acronyms, the LOLs, the LMAOs (or its longer, dopier offshoot ROFLMAO).

Rarely, if ever, are they used honestly, because, really, who laughs out loud that often or actually gets on the floor and rolls around while laughing? Their overuse helps drive up the annoyance factor, and there are no signs of them stopping anytime soon.

One newish one, however, must be stopped immediately: FML.

For the fortunate uniformed, FML is short for "Fuck My Life."

I've yet to meet anyone who actually deserved to use FML, mainly because most people who qualify for it aren't spending their days on Facebook or Twitter. When I was in Haiti, for instance, not one child (even the ones who were clearly starving) offered up a single use of FML. Anne Frank didn't write, "Dear Diary, yet another day hiding from the Nazis and trying to avoid being savagely murdered. FML."

Perhaps I've just reached the Andy Rooney Category, but I'm afraid we're turning into a nation of whiners more obsessed with complaining about our lives than we are with trying to do anything about it. It's easier to post emo-rific status updates followed by FML than it is to actively question yourself with "What can I do to improve this situation?"

I know that each generation looks at the next with certain levels of distaste, just like my parents looked at grunge music and gangster rap in the mid-1990s, but this just seems a tad different. My generation might have been comprised of slackers who did nothing, but I fully believe that it's today's youth who not only do nothing, they also then complain about how they've been so emotionally scarred by someone they may never be able to do anything again. Then, of course, they write it about via social networking. If we are Generation X, then they're Generation Ehh.

I guess this is the point where I shake my fist at the kids and their damned Internets, but I'm really not trying to be a cantankerous old man. What I'd like is for people, particularly those my age or older who have started embracing this FML ideology, to try to take a few moments and realize that maybe, just maybe, life isn't quite as bad you might think. Yes, some bad things befall us from time to time, but that's part of life (and for heaven's sake, please stop treating Facebook like your own personal journal). Maybe we can all try some personal accountability at making ourselves happy. Maybe we can even reach out to others who might need a lift, actually using social networking to, you know, network. And maybe then, we'll stop being quite so soft and spoiled, so weak and whiny and put FML away for good.

If not, well, then I guess we're all effed.

THE DEAD ON BLACK RIVER

By Aaron Saylor

It's snowing again.

We check the thick knot, each of us, and lock the yellow rope around my waist. A quick tug on the lifeline convinces me it'll hold. I sure as hell hope it holds, anyway; we've come too far and lost too much to turn back now.

I tell Lenny, "Let's do this," but instead of doing anything, we just stand there in the chilled January night. Neither of us says a word, though eventually, we manage nervous little laughs, spitting icicles at each other's face.

Finally, when we can put it off no longer, Lenny takes his end of the rope and lowers me over the cliff's edge, towards the frozen Black River below.

My descent moves in quick stutters, five or six feet at a time. Lenny stands his ground against my solid buck eighty and manages enough control that he keeps me from plunging towards the ice that waits underneath me. I appreciate that.

The ice. Goddamn, that ice. Here in the heart of winter, that ice looks more like asphalt than anything else, cold and dark and solid, so solid, just waiting down there for the next poor fool to splat down on its unforgiving surface. If I crash from this height – thirty, maybe forty feet – I'd break a leg for sure, or my back, or my neck. Maybe all of that and then some. At the least, my skull would split open and bloody brains would splash out and I'd have no choice but to lay there in them, because while the fall might kill me, it would surely take its sweet time. I'd land in about two seconds and lay there for an hour or more, two hours, a day, who knows? How much time might pass before my body succumbs to its injuries? I've gotten myself in pretty good shape these last few months, on the run like we've been, so who knows what this ol' boy could take?

But odds are it wouldn't be the injuries that got me anyway. Eventually, the fuckers would come. Lenny couldn't help. And they would come. They'd come, and hopefully I'd already be dead when they got there. I don't want to go through that. God knows I don't want to be awake when they start gnawing on me.

You think about things like that out here.

After touching down on the surface of the ice, I look up and signal Lenny that I'm OK. Hopefully he can see my hand waving in the full moonlight. We can't yell out to each other – human voices bring the fuckers running, we learned that lesson a long time ago, the shitty way – but soon enough I see his hand wave back. Right after that, he pulls the rope up.

He couldn't handle the drop so we came up with this plan: Lenny would lower me to the ice, then scale down the cliff-side and catch up with me up river. After that, we'd head towards the mountains and hopefully find a place to rest before sunrise. Seems like dumb luck has brought us to a place that's not yet been overrun by those damn half-deaders, so there's a good chance that if we can get to the mountains we can last another few days. I'll take that. A few days is a hell of a long time in this world. We can worry about later, later.

For now, though, here I am, alone on the Black River, waiting for my friend to catch up. I hope he does.

Both sides of the riverbank open out toward the snowy plain. I look around as I trudge through the snow, expecting the shadows of undead things swaying in the winter breeze, their blank silver eyes fixated on me, those soulless shades waiting for the right moment to lurch forward out of the darkness...

I don't see anything, though. That means they still haven't caught up to us.

But they will. Sooner or later, they will.

Off to the north I continue. Lenny thought north was the right way to go and I couldn't think of any reason to disagree with that. Go north far enough and eventually we'll hit the mountains; if we can get there, we'll have the high ground and maybe a puncher's chance at survival for more than a few weeks. That's a big If, sure – and there will no doubt be a lot more Ifs to face between here and there – but this is the world now.

This is this.

Snow and ice crunch beneath my feet, the only sound in this dead midnight. For a second it occurs to me that the sound might be so loud it blows my cover, brings the fuckers shambling across the frozen plain like fire ants on a picnic blanket, only much slower and much, much nastier. And hungrier. And deader.

Can't think about that right now, though. I shake away the rotting thoughts, zip my collar up to my chin, and keep going.

Keep going.

Keep going.

Keep going.

See, the thing is, with the ways of the world nowadays, a man's got to do everything he can to make sure he's always moving forward. That's something Lenny and me figured out a long time ago. This great state of Montana – and every other state in the Union, judging by what I could pick up from the radio before it finally bit the big one – is full up now with dead folks come back to life and it's just like we all saw in the movies – they just keep on comin'. Call them whatever you want. Zombies, undead, monsters, walkers, reanimates. They don't stop, they don't sleep, they just keep on keepin' on, until the time comes that you put them down or they put you down, whichever happens first. And if you stop in one place for too long, all you do is make it easy on them. You go from moving target to sitting duck and it's them doing the putting and you doing the down.

That might be eyes over there.

I could swear…

The wind just kicked up a churn of snow and I could swear that for a second there were two silver eyes out there, glinting like dollar coins in the dark. At least two. Maybe four. Maybe ten. Hell, maybe a hundred. It's like they say about cockroaches: wherever you see one there are ten thousand you don't see.

Not feeling safe at all, I reach for the .45 strapped to my side. Even in this heavy parka, I can still feel the weight of the weapon against my belt. That's real comfort, let me tell you. A comfort I never appreciated in the old days, back before all the shit happened. Sometimes I feel like it's the only comfort I'll ever find in this world we wander, no matter if I live to be a hundred years old. Which of course, I won't.

Straight ahead, I can see the mountains, their peaks sharp silhouettes against a crisp and starry backdrop. The Black River winds towards them on flat land for a good two miles before it turns into a valley between two of the slopes. Assuming all goes as planned, that's where I get off the ice, find some cover and wait for Lenny. That's where we meet up. If we last that long.

I remember the first time I saw one of the fuckers out here.

Now, I'm not talking about the first one *ever*. I couldn't even guess about that. I've seen so damn many thousands of 'em since those demon days when everything got pear-shaped on us that it's one big mishmash of rotted flesh. I remember when the world came unhinged and there were hundreds of 'em clogging up the streets, ripping up any poor soul that stumbled into their path. That was pure bat shit fucking crazy – I ain't saying it wasn't bat shit crazy– but to be honest it wasn't really that different from anything folks saw in the average apocalypse movie back when apocalypse movies seemed so absurd and impossible. But the impossible came to life: people clawing over each other to get away even as hordes of walking corpses tore them all to bloody hell. The screams. The blood. The ripping flesh. The desperate cries for mercy. Pretty much everything you'd expect when the long lost dead rose to reclaim their places among the living. In those days, I saw it all. I saw children eat their parents, mothers eat their sons, wives eat their husbands, husbands eat themselves. I really did. I saw a bearded old man in a wheelchair chew up his own fingers and spit them out on the sidewalk. Really, I did. I saw a little blonde-haired girl claw her eyes out with a flathead screwdriver. I saw two dogs fight a coyote for a dead goat; I saw a dead goat fight two dogs for a coyote. No kidding, I did, I saw that. Just like I saw a guy in a pink fuzzy bathrobe split his head open with a crowbar. I saw a lonesome horse wandering an empty street with his guts ripped out, slung over his back like a riding blanket. I saw the vultures circling. God, did I see the vultures circling, circling, their beady eyes glued to the earth below in a never-ending search for the comfort of carrion. I saw all that, and then some. But that's not what I'm talking about now.

I'm talking about the first time I saw one of the half-dead *out here*, in the wild. After all the shit went down and things kind of took on their own new normalcy. After the world got a hell of a lot quieter. It's a hushed planet now, after all, with ninety-nine point nine percent of the human race shredded. To be honest, I kind of miss the noise – the aimless conversations, the honking horns, the roar of jets overhead, the steady thump of jackhammers on concrete.

You think about things like that out here.

We'd ducked inside the mouth of a cave somewhere in Idaho for what I hoped would be one of the few decent rest stops we got since taking off on our long run. It's become a grand joke between us, the name we've given this life, the Long Run. As in, it's so damn long, it ain't ever gonna end. Ever. *Ever.*

That day, the sun was just starting its dawn jaint, but there wasn't much daylight to speak about with a solid sheet of gray clouds above us. A fog blanket hugged the ground and looked like it would be there for a while, thanks to a soft rain that drizzled interminable. The land seemed so… peaceful. There's nothing else I can call it except peaceful. The fog, the whispering raindrops, the soft grass, the damp ground beneath us. Quiet enough to make you forget just where it was you came from, and where it was you were going.

Just inside the cave, Lenny was stone asleep on the dirt, out of it like he'd not had a decent sleep in a month which, now that I think about it, he probably hadn't.

I sat cross-legged nearby, staring out at the steady precipitation, when an awful moan floated up from outside, below us, a pitiful wail so wracked with pain that I had no desire to see its origin. Of course, I also knew that I had to find the source of the wail. And worse, I had to put a stop to it. If it – whatever *it* was – kept up that racket then sure as hell the fuckers would come calling.

Our cave loomed halfway up a shaggy hillside that was littered with briar bushes and fallen tree limbs. I stood up, walked out into the rain, and peered down the incline. Near the bottom of the hill was the source of the cry: a young elk, laid over on its side, eyes half closed, mouth open, pink tongue rolled out. The animal was dying, I could see that for sure. But it wasn't dead yet.

Then, I realized: it wasn't the elk making such a hideous sound.

It was something else entirely.

I could see an old woman down there. What used to be an old woman, anyway. What I *couldn't* see was another living corpse, which surprised me. It was just her. Like I said, this was the first time for me. Up until then, our experience with the half-dead consisted entirely of trying to avoid whatever clusters of them appeared in our vicinity.

But there was no cluster here. Just this one, all by herself, like she'd left the herd and struck out on her own.

This old woman, now let me tell you, she was a tick past dead. Several ticks. She wore her diamond-blue funeral dress; with its lace collar, the dress looked like something out of the 1940's. Her hair was mostly rotted off, save for a couple of ratty wisps that fluttered in the wind. A necklace of pearls dangled from her bony neck, probably the pearls her husband bought on their fortieth wedding anniversary or some shit like that, then buried them with her because he was afraid his crazy brother-in-law would rob the house for his sister's jewelry. You think about these things out here.

The dead woman pulled back from the elk's belly, her face covered in gore, blood and entrails dripping off her teeth, her jaws, her chin.

And she moaned.

That moan. It jitters my spine just thinking about it now. The moan of the dead, the moan of the lost, the moan of the hungry. The sullen cry you wish you could hurry up and forget as soon as you've heard it, even though you know you'll remember it for the rest of your sorry life. That moan. God, that moan.

She leaned forward, and bit a hunk out of the elk's throat the same way a little kid would take a bite out of a ripe tomato.

I retreated into the cave and puked, a foot or so from Lenny's head. That woke him up.

"What's going on?" he said.

Wiping flecks of vomit from my mouth, I felt the awkward sensation of shame crawl up my chest. We'd seen plenty worse on the Run, but for whatever reason, the guts dripping of that one dead old lady's chin just struck me the wrong way.

"What the hell's going on, Jake?" Lenny asked one more time.

"We got a visitor."

He sat up straight, rubbed his fingers through his dirty hair. "Don't tell me it's one of them –"

I told him. "It's one of them, Get up now. You know how it is. Those things are like cockroaches, if you see one there's ten thousand behind it."

Lenny climbed to his feet, stepped out of the cave and peered down the hillside. He looked left, looked right, then out towards the horizon.

"I just see the one," he said, unimpressed. "One half-dead motherfucker."

"There could be more."

"I just see the one."

"Fine. Whatever," I said. "Unless you wanna take the chance, we gotta get goin'." I grabbed my .306 from its leaning spot on the cold cave wall – this is when I used to favor a rifle, back before I decided rifles were too much weight for the Run – and loaded it with a cartridge from my jacket pocket.

A few seconds later, I had the un-deceased's skull in my crosshairs. One squeeze of the trigger and her head exploded in a sick shower that reminded me of beef stew. I hadn't eaten beef stew in almost a year and the last time I did it gave me a severe case of food poisoning because my girlfriend let the meat sit out on the countertop for too long. You think about these things out here.

I walk on Black River, straight towards the mountains. The snow falls heavier now, and even worse, the wind has picked up. I won't lose my way – the ice will steer me right to the mountains – but with the white stuff swirling around like this, visibility's down to a quarter-mile at best. It would be hard to spot one of those silver-eyed bastards before he was damn near on top of me, and then it would be too late. There'd be no running away in this weather.

I take a quick look behind me, on the irrational hope that I might see Lenny back there. Instead I peer into a billion little flakes dancing around in a million different directions. The moonlight creates just enough glare to make things worse; I might as well be looking for a raindrop in a bubble bath.

Then, from one side, I hear what sounds like a shovel being dragged through the snow.

Someone is walking nearby.

Not someone. Something.

I jerk my head to one side, just in time to see a vaguely human figure stagger out of the snow. The thought occurs to me: *this is it. You guys had a good long run, but it's over now.* For just a second I feel a sense of peace, knowing that I'll finally get to let go of everything.

The figure shambles closer, but it struggles to cut through the wind. The thing is coming for me, but the wind won't cooperate. Keeps blowing him off course.

That gives me the opportunity to regain my senses.

My pistol.

I fumble for the gun, and fire a wild shot KRA-KOW in the direction of oncoming traffic. A white plume skits off behind my pursuer. The bullet ricochets off the ground and disappears harmless into the night.

I lift the gun higher. It's hard to get a steady aim in this wind, but I manage to sight down the figure's head, or at least what I think is the head given the fact that I can't really see much of anything. Even if I miss again, I'm not going down with any bullets left in the chamber, you can count on that.

"Hold on! Hold on, goddammit!" the thing yells, waving both arms like he's trying to flag down a 747.

What did it say?

"Put the damn gun down!"

That sounds like Lenny.

"Is that you, Lenny?"

"Hell yeah it's me! I said I'd catch up to you, didn't I?"

I lower the .45 and stand there, waiting for him to catch up the rest of the way. After a couple more minutes, he does.

When he's standing right in front of me, I say, "I could have killed you, dumbass. What happened to meeting in the mountains?"

"I caught up, that's what happened," he says with a shrug. That's the thing about Lenny. He's matter-of-fact, was that way when I met him singing karaoke in a bar a few years ago, and he's stayed that way even now, through it all.

His parka hood is pulled tight, but still the snow has managed to accumulate on his face. He wipes that free and says, "Gotta find us some cover. We can't walk in this shit for too long."

Matter of fact, he's right. "Where?"

"There's an old shack just over there." He motions towards the river's edge. "I passed it on my way. Can't be more than a couple hundred yards back. I say we go there, wait out the storm, then pick back up when the weather clears."

The idea of backtracking doesn't hold much appeal, but the truth is, we don't have much of a choice. If we fight this weather for too long, we won't have to worry about being chewed on by starving zombies, because the snowstorm will freeze our bodies solid before anything else gets a go at us.

So, I nod my head. Lenny ambles off towards this shack he's discovered, and I follow.

Ten minutes later, we reach our destination. It's a wreck, not that I expected anything else. The structure appears cobbled together from spare parts, mismatched boards nailed together at obtuse angles, with pieces of tin sheet used to fill the most haphazard gaps. There aren't many straight lines. The roof is sheet metal, curled up at one corner, flapping in the winter wind. There are no windows, but a plywood door hangs for dear life on its frame.

I see a light.

An orange glow flickers around the edges of the door. It's neither bright nor steady, but it's there.

"Is that a candle?" I ask Lenny.

"Looks like somebody's home," he says.

"Were they home when you came by a few minutes ago?"

"I don't know. I didn't notice."

We stand there, looking at it.

Lenny says, "You think we should check it out?"

I shrug my shoulders and step forward. About that time, a big wind kicks up and the door swings open. We can see inside.

We can see *who* is inside.

A man. A shabby man, seated at a crude wooden table, with one candle lit before him that casts blinks of light around the tiny room. He's swathed in tattered blankets, his head poking out the top. When the door blows open, he doesn't move. He just stares at us. The awful weather invades his space and he doesn't move, not a bit, except to reach out and draw his candle closer. Other than that, he sits there at his little table, and stares at us.

Lenny realizes a couple of beats before I do that we've happened upon another human being. While I'm still processing my thoughts – *Jee-sus! Is this real? Out here? Jee-sus!* – he takes off for the door, stomps up the rickety steps, catches one foot on the bottom of door frame, and trips into the shack.

The man in the blankets still doesn't move.

Less than a minute later, I'm in there with them, pulling the door closed behind me and latching it (barely) on a metal hook in the wall. Lenny stands and brushes the snow from his clothes.

Now I'm trying to sort out this new situation but not finding many answers. Good answers, anyway. I'll be damned if this ain't a peculiar sight. You just don't find many humans anymore, and almost never outside of the cities; we've seen one human face beside Lenny's in the last six months, a beardy Mexican who was working his way back to California to see if he could find his two children. (Good luck with that, *mi amigo*.) The few folks left alive tend to stay huddled in urban areas, scavenging what food they can from store shelves and empty houses, eating rats and dogs and whatever other animals they might catch. Not many have the requisite skills for tracking real game, which is why Lenny and I prefer travelling in the wild – less competition out here. Fewer monsters, too; ruined cities teem with the rot of lumbering death, but it's not as bad when you get further off the roads. Vigilance is always the rule, but there isn't quite the sense of resigned doom that prevails under the streetlights. We average a decent meal every couple of days. The deer and rabbit populations haven't suffered the same decline as humans, though I suspect the dead will probably turn on them once *homo sapiens* peters to its eventual quiet end.

"You okay, friend?" Lenny says to the man at the table. Lenny tends to be more positive than me. I would never assume a stranger is my friend.

The man says nothing, still doesn't move. He just stares at us.

I whisper, "Let's leave him be –"

Lenny takes a couple more steps towards the table.

"Welcome," says the man.

Lenny jumps back. I jump back. We both reach for our firearms, but before either of us can draw down, the man rises from his seat, ragged blankets still draped around his shoulders.

And he smiles.

He smiles.

Those teeth –

Those teeth!

Too late, I realize we've walked into a trap. This is not just another person that we've stumbled across here. It's not your average everyday reanimated corpse, either. No, what we've got on our hands now is neither alive nor dead, and probably hasn't been for a few hundred years. This is, in the parlance of our twisted times, a bloodsucker. No question about it.

As if to offer final confirmation, the vampire opens his mouth, and with a demonic gleam shows us the two sharp fangs protruding from his top row of teeth. He steps out from behind the table, coming towards us slow but with purpose, as if he knows there's not a thing in the world we can do to stop him, which there isn't. We're fucked. I know we're fucked. Lenny knows we're fucked. We're fucked. I don't take my eyes off this creature. I'm hoping for a miracle, but expecting that we've finally reached the end of our Long Run.

I'm staring down the vampire, waiting for him to leap forward and rip my throat out, when to my complete shock, Lenny grabs the candle from the table and sets fire to the motherfucker's blanket. The blanket goes up like tinder; flames engulf the fiend before he can do anything to stop them. I'd always heard that when you touch even the smallest flame to a vampire, he'll go up like brown leaves in dry season, but I'd also hoped never to find out for sure. Now I know.

The fire shoots towards the ceiling. The bloodsucker screams, a high-pitched scream straight out of the bowels of hell. Lenny and I burst out into the snowstorm and don't look back.

We escape on the solid ice of Black River, moving faster than we have in weeks. It's a struggle, keeping our balance in the blowing snow and wind, but we do our best.

For the first time, I glance over my shoulder and deep orange flames already licking around the rooftop corners of the vampire's shack. Soon they will grow to full blaze, and the beacon in the stark winter night will bring together scores of the dead from across the wintry plain. There's nothing we can do about that now except hope to outrun them.

It's not a comforting thought.

Then, just when I turn my head back up river, towards the mountains, Lenny trips and goes down. We stop long enough for me to help him back his feet, then we're on the Long Run again, kicking up little clumps of snow in our wake.

When we get to the mountains, we manage to find some quick cover under a few fallen fir trees. Neither one of us says anything for two hours. Sometimes there's just nothing left to say, right? Right. Not when you're living in a world where the dead feast on the living. Not when you see the things that we have seen. After all, I saw a little blonde-haired girl claw her eyes out with a flathead screwdriver. I saw two dogs fight a coyote for a dead goat. I saw a dead goat fight two dogs for a coyote. I saw the buzzards circling. God, I saw the buzzards circling.

If I looked up, I bet I'd see them circling over my head right now.

Finally, Lenny chimes in with a simple, "Can you believe that shit? He burned like gasoline on newspaper. "

"He did. I was there. I believe it."

"I thought we were done. Didn't know if that candle would be enough."

"You saved our asses, Lenny. I never expected to see a bloodsucker out here –"

"Me, neither. They weren't supposed to be this far west."

"It looks like they're this far west."

"What do you think this all means?"

"I don't know. What do you think it means?"

"I think it means… " His words trail off. He takes a deep breath, exhales through his nose. "I'm not really sure."

He doesn't have to tell me. We both know what this means – that this long run just got a helluva lot longer. It's bad enough, always keeping both eyes open for that next living dead flesh-eater that waits around the corner. Truth is, over the months we've actually gotten used to the zombies, or used to them as can be, anyway; they're relatively slow and you can put them down easy enough with a sharp blow to the head. Just like in the movies.

But these vampires, who knows what this is going to be like. For now, I assume they'll be close to the popular portrayal, too, which means Lenny and me need to get our hands on some wooden stakes, crosses, silver if we can find any. Hell, if we're lucky, there might be some garlic left on one grocery shelf or another somewhere between here and the Pacific Ocean.

These won't be mindless dogs, either. We've already seen that they're smart enough to set a trap and we're just dumb enough to fall into it. It's a new ballgame now.

"Zombies. Vampires. Jesus Christ," says Lenny. "What's next, werewolves?"

On cue, a howl echoes across the mountainside. It's distant, and not any different than any other howl we've heard on other cold nights like this, when the moon hangs full and the snow kicks across the frozen plain. It could be any kind of wolf, maybe a coyote, maybe a feral house dog. It doesn't have to be a werewolf.

But you never know.

Lenny says, "I'll take watch first," and I'm in no shape to argue with him. I lay back against the soft needles of the fallen fir tree and close my eyes, telling tales to myself that this will be the night when I finally get some sleep. Already I imagine dead, silvery eyes closing in on us, even as my own eyelids barely flutter closed. You think about these things out here. If you stop in one place for too long, all you do is make it easy on them. It's going to be a long night here with Lenny, a long night wondering what other monsters wait for us in the darkness. Another long night on the long, long run.

Is Being Good All It's Cracked Up to Be?

by Kevin Hall

I've done my best to live the right way / I get up every morning and go to work each day ...

I try to be a good person.

And it's starting to kill me.

I have a bit of a Jesus complex in which I try to absorb the pain of those closest to me rather than see them suffer. In most cases, I would gladly sacrifice my own well-being to help them feel better.

It doesn't always work, though.

Sometimes I feel ignored. Other times I feel like people take advantage of my goodwill. I think that might have happened this weekend. I'm not sure. Either way, I found myself in a position in which I should have walked away, leaving my sanity somewhat safer. Instead, I dove headfirst into the situation, sacrificing myself to help a friend (an ex-girlfriend, actually) who was hurting.

Now, it's hurting me, and I can't help myself. Maybe that's why I'm writing, using this blog as a cathartic experience. I don't know. I guess maybe I'm hoping someone, anyone, out there will have something to suggest, some simple piece of advice that will make sense.

But your eyes go blind and your blood runs cold / Sometimes I feel so weak I just want to explode ...

I should point out that I'm not always good. I guess maybe a truly good person doesn't really have to try, but I never said I succeeded at being good. I merely try.

Some days I fail. I'll admit that I can be the meanest son-of-a-bitch you've ever known, saying things that cut to the deepest core of your weaknesses. And I'd be lying if I said I didn't sometimes enjoy that. Hell, when those words come spilling out, it feels good. It always does.

But it doesn't last.

It never does.

Explode and tear this whole town apart/Take a knife and cut this pain from my heart/Find somebody itching for something to start …

I guess I'm just glad I'm feeling something. I spent about three years on anti-depressants, during which time I truly felt no emotions. I gave them up four years ago, and since then, I'm just a walking ball of emotions, feeling high levels of everything. I've taken some major steps to rein everything in, but still, some people have suggested that I take it even further by reducing my connections to so many emotions.

I'm afraid, though, that such a move would change everything about me. These emotions make me want to be a better person, a better friend, a better boyfriend, a better son, a better brother, a better co-worker, a better everything.

But where do you draw the line? At what point do I just say, "That's not my problem" and let you take care of your own mess?
I'm not sure I can.

More importantly, I'm not sure I want to.

The dogs on Main Street howl 'cause they understand/If I could take one moment into my hands …

I live in a world where I'm taught to love everyone else. At my church, Faith Baptist in Georgetown, we believe in a mission to out-love the world, focusing less on fire and brimstone and eternal damnation and more on what we can do to make the world a better place by loving everyone. We're definitely a "do unto others" type of congregation.

So, I guess if you believe in God (I do) and heaven (ditto), then it all pays off in the end. And every so often, little things happen every day to make you realize it might all be worthwhile in the here and now. Today, for instance, I came home from work to discover my neighbor had mowed my grass without expecting any compensation in return. "It's just what neighbors do," he told me.

I needed that.

In one simple gesture, this man I've known for all of two months made a profound difference in my day, lifting my spirits (and making my yard look fantastic). There's nothing wrong with giving of yourself. There's nothing wrong with being a good neighbor, both literally and figuratively.

Mister I ain't a boy, no I'm a man/ And I believe in the promised land.

I guess I just want to believe more in that good things happen to good people. Light triumphs over darkness. Luke Skywalker not only destroys the Death Star but ultimately helps redeem Darth Vader, the epitome of evil. These things happen over time, though. Rome wasn't built in a day, after all, and Vader wasn't saved until *Return of the Jedi*.

I believe the payoffs will come, both in this life and the next. Call it karma. Call it fate. Call it divine intervention. Call it whatever you wish, but it will come. Maybe it will be in the form of The Right Woman, or maybe it will be a healthy, happy life for my three nephews, or maybe it will be something I can't even imagine at this point in my life. I don't know. Frankly, I don't care. I just know that it will happen. And right now, that's good enough for me.

FOREVER YOUNG

by Kevin Hall

Their teenage voices hummed in unison, a soft buzz at first, barely audible. After 10 seconds or so – there was no exact science to it; these were evil geniuses, sure, but they were still teenagers, and really, plans at that age are uncool, man – the steady hum would grow, bit by bit, until the entire room provided a constant noise ready to drive the old man insane.

The old man, though, couldn't hear it. Not at first, at least.

Which, I guess, was the point.

By the time he finally noticed it, the humming would occasionally be peppered with giggles as the teens tried (and failed) to contain their amusement. He looked puzzled.

"Class, can anyone here that?" he'd ask.

"Hear what?" somehow would question back with the type of mock sincerity perfected by high school sophomores across America.

He would fiddle with his hearing aid, turning knobs until he found the setting he needed, then he returned to his duties.

The class, of course, returned to its duties, which primarily consisted of tormenting this poor old man. They would speak in low whispers, causing him to again adjust his hearing aid, this time turning the volume up.

By then it was too late. The class would start talking in loud voices, almost shouts, that probably deafened an already near-deaf man. As his hearing aid boomed from the voices, the class erupted with laughter, another oh-so-clever practical joke successfully completed.

He was Mr. Young.

We were the class.

He was, without a doubt, the kindest, sweetest, most sincere substitute teacher in the history of Powell County, if not Kentucky, if not the United States. I can't speak for other countries.

We were, without a doubt, assholes.

We should all hang our heads in shame.

Anyone who attended a Powell County school any time in the 1990s (and probably in the 1980s) got treated to the substitute teaching of Mr. Young, a retired minister who was in his 80s (at least) in my time. He might have even been pushing 90. It's quite possible, and it's not surprising. The man was a machine.

I mean that quite literally, of course.

We all remember Mr. Young's "typewriter," which was, in hindsight, the most awesomely awesome thing any substitute teacher has done. I don't even need to use hindsight to know this. We sat there spellbound when he did it, knowing full well that this trick was both corny and entertaining (but mostly entertaining).

For the unlucky uninitiated (which can pretty much only be Powell Countians younger than 23 and non-PCers), Mr. Young's typewriter consisted of him making clacking sounds by rattling his false teeth in his mouth while his fingers typed in mid-air. Once he got to the end of the "page," he would place one finger to the side of his nose, making a inhaling honking noise while he turned his head back to his left, thus allowing the typing to continue.

Keeping up with then-modern technology, Mr. Young upgraded to an electric printer, somehow wiggling his ear while either humming or getting his hearing aid to make a noise. It's not that I can't remember the detail of how he made it happen; I've willfully blocked it. Then and now, it was the work of magic. I'm pretty sure that if he were alive today, he'd have upgraded technology and do some sort of e-mail via WiFi, but only after also showing kids the typewriter.

If that wasn't enough to make you immediately love him and realize his total goodness, Mr. Young was a retired minister, a fact many of his students did not know. I counted myself one of the fortunate ones, even catching him in oratory action a few times when he would guest preach at the First Presbyterian Church of Stanton.

You have no idea what it's like to be 10 years old at church, only to see Mr. Young as your substitute teacher. I would get absolutely giddy, telling my grandparents "You will not believe what you're about to see," as I sat spellbound wondering the eternal question: would he do the typewriter trick?

He never did, and although I failed to understand why as a child, I can see now that a stoic Presbyterian church might not be the most appropriate place for Vaudeville-style humor. Actually, that's not true at all – I still think he should have performed for the congregation, perhaps as the offering was being taken. It was definitely worth more than a tithe.

Mr. Young died a few years back, and Powell County's schools are worse off for it. I'm not sure how much we learned during the days Mr. Young would serve as our sub other than new ways to play pranks, which is a shame. I think, though, that even then, we knew we should feel bad about the little jokes, but when you're 15, you pretty much feel powerless to stop the wave, so you press on, even at the expense of a kind old man.

So now, here I am, 34, with a fully formed conscience that today sits feeling a bit guilty. I think we all should. We were just kids then, but we're adults now, so today, I say this (and I encourage you to join me): Mr. Young, on behalf of Powell County, I'm sorry.

And knowing Mr. Young, he would forgive us.

Then he'd do the typewriter trick.

THE DAY I FULLY EMBRACED MY AGE WHILE SIMULTANEOUSLY STICKING IT TO THE AARP

by Kevin Hall

I arrived home yesterday to a piece of mail that made Tuesday, Aug. 22, 2011, officially, the Happiest Day of My Life, a combination of all three of my nephews' births, my wedding day and my divorce day, college graduation and my second-, third- and fourth-favorite Christmases ever.

In my hands was something I had declined last year but now had the chance to rectify the situation, an opportunity I shan't again let pass.

I had an AARP membership application.

I should probably use this time to note that I'm 35, and while I'm five weeks away from turning 36, I'm still a good 14 years and five weeks away from turning 50, which just so happens to be the AARP membership age.

I read the letter, read, re-read, re-re-read and re-re-re-read the fine print (given the target audience of the AARP, you'd think the fine print wouldn't be quite so fine), and I saw nothing, not one word, mind you, that said anything at all about a need to, you know, be retired to actually be a member of the American Association of Retired Persons or, at the very least, close to retirement age.

To be perfectly honest, while I care about the needs of our aging population (things like Medicaid or Medicare, whichever one is for old people), I care much more, in the short term, for things like the amazing AARP discounts. Members get immediate savings on restaurants, stores and hotels (the hotel savings alone are worth the cost of the membership), and even though some have strict stipulations (Denny's, for instance, gives 20 percent off, but only between the hours of 4 and 10 p.m.), overall, the value was staggering.

I faced a few immediate decisions in filling out my application, most notably being how long did I want to be a member, with options of one, three and five years. Personally, I think it's a bit of a gamble for AARPers to select the five-year membership since a) they're old; and b) might not live another five years. When you might reach your personal expiration date before your membership card does, you might want to select a shorter plan.

On the other hand, one year at $16 didn't seem like a good enough value, so I opted to split the difference, settling on three years for $43 (or $14.33 annually). I wrote my check, placed the prepaid return envelope in my mailbox and waited for the good times to starting rolling.

I explained all of this to a friend, who immediately questioned my ability to join an organization designed specifically for the elder members of our society. She put it in simple terms: "Kevin, you're not old enough to join that."

"I can join the NAACP, and I'm not C," I countered. "I'm barely even a P."

Despite making what I believed to be a valid argument, one that even the Supreme Court would have to uphold, I began Wednesday morning with a few doubts. While I remained confident in that my membership application said absolutely nothing in the negative about my being 35, I still felt like someone somewhere was going to swoop down on me and accuse me of not being old enough (which while technically true remains not my fault since I had a pre-approved membership application).

Not wanting to risk the wrath of The United States Secretary of Scary Old People Who Can Put Young Whippersnappers and Wiseacres in Their Places (I think we'd all be in agreement that Wilford Brimley has a lifetime appointment in this position), I got on the AARP's website to do some research.

Again, nothing seemed to contradict my long-standing belief (OK, so one-day-standing belief) that I was eligible to be an AARP member solely because they had invited me to become one. I decided to test the system by filling out another application, knowing I could cancel out on the confirmation page.

One problem: instead of providing a final look-see at the information prior to confirmation, the AARP membership application just goes directly to the "Congratulations, you are now a member" page.

First off, see: I can't operate a computer! I'm clearly eligible to be in the AARP.

Second of all, I would suggest the AARP, which up to that point has the most elderly person-friendly website I've ever seen, not jump straight from "enter your payment method" to "Congratulations, you are now a member." Speaking on behalf of all AARP-eligible persons throughout this country, the extra step wouldn't kill you, but it might induce some panic-stricken heart attacks among us.

To make sure I hadn't fouled up the system, I called the toll-free number to make sure I wasn't going to have separate memberships. An older-type woman answered the phone to assist me (I think her name was Peggy, which sounds like the absolute perfect name to be answering calls on the AARP hotline), and in resolving The Case of the Multiple Memberships (to be fair, I think she just flipped ahead to the end of the book and read the upside-down answers), she casually mentioned that I would be getting an "associate membership" since "you don't sound like you're 50."

Uh-oh. I don't like this smart mouth on Peggy.

"Um, what exactly is the difference between a membership and an associate membership?" I asked.

"An associate member gets access to the magazine."

"No discounts?"

"No, no discounts. You only get the magazine."

"So, to be clear, I'd be paying $43 for three years worth of the AARP magazine and get none of the discounts?"

"That's correct. You'll be an associate member until you're 50."

I thanked Peggy for her help and asked to speak to a supervisor.

After being on hold for 15 minutes, the supervisor, Tammy (again, perfectly named), got on the phone with about the kindest voice I've ever heard outside of a Cracker Barrel. This is smart business on the AARP's part: I can't get overly angry at a grandmotherly type.

Except, of course, when this grandmotherly type is trying to gyp me. If that's the case, let the anger commence.

I stayed calm, though, and explained my case, using phrases like:

"So, even though the literature says nothing about a so-called 'associate membership,' you'll still take my $43, send me a monthly magazine and pretend everything is OK?"

"This sounds like a scam."

"I'm having a hard time seeing how this is legal."

Tammy explained to me that I had erroneously received the pre-approved membership.

"It's usually targeted mailing," she said, "and it really shouldn't have reached you."

Let's pause for a minute to address the fact I'm on a targeted mailing list from the AAFRP (and Mom, yes, I'm afraid the "F" stands for exactly what you think the "F" stands for, but in this case, it's totally justified, much like when you used to say "sht"). Some might find this insulting; I find it liberating. I do certain things in my life to accentuate my youthfulness, so why not embrace the other side?

But back to Tammy …

"That's the thing, though – I did receive it, and I think it's only fair that it be honored," I told her.

She paused. "You're right."

I literally got cold chills (although, to be fair, it might have just been a draft blowing through at work; I'm in the AARP now – I get chilled easily).

Tammy told me she would delete my date of birth, thus allowing me to have a full membership. She took my credit card information, gave me the website to access my temporary card and said she would be talking to the marketing department to advise them to do include an age-related disclaimer on the future applications.

I thanked her and told her I would be an AARP member for life. "I hope to one day be 50," I explained.

She laughed and said that's an admirable goal. This Tammy was a bit of a flirt; I thought about asking for her number, maybe taking her for a bite at Morrison's Cafeteria, but I let the moment pass. Maybe I'll catch her some other time, perhaps at Del Boca Vista.

Now, though, I have bigger things to consider since I'm an AARP member. I have discounts to use, and, frankly, a cause in which to fight. I will stand up for the rights of my fellow AARPers. We will not be swept aside by a younger generation in their skinny jeans and bad haircuts.

No, we will fight.

I will fight.

I will fight for my right to party, particularly at reasonable hours with music at a respectable level and with plans to clean up the mess afterward.

I'm in the AARP, and that's how we roll.

THIS IS WHY WE DON'T TAKE FAMILY VACATIONS

by Kevin Hall

In roughly 40 hours, I will be surrounded by sand and ocean, leaving my worries (the non-family variety) at home. Come Saturday afternoon, the only things that will really matter to me are the following words: beach, seafood and vacation.

This is assuming, of course, that we actually get there.

My family (and when I say family, I mean pretty much the entire family as there are 13 of us going) and I are heading to a beach in North Carolina, marking the first time I've gone on a beach vacation since I was (I think) 7. This is a piece of history, I guess. It's also a bit of a risk.

The last beach vacation, taken 28 years ago, didn't go very well.

Dad had new tires put on our truck and camper the week before we were to leave for Myrtle Beach. If you don't know Doc Hall, you should know this is not a man who leaves things to chance. Tires get checked. Oil gets changed. Driving routes get mapped. Order gets maintained. Everything gets in its right place ahead of time, ensuring a smooth vacation the rest of the time.

This is important to know.

Somewhere in Tennessee, a man drove past us, giving the "you have a flat tire" signal as he did so (yes, kids, people used to actually signal to other drivers to let them know a tire was going flat or that a light was out). Dad shook his head at the guy, knowing a flat on the new tires was impossible. Still, though, he stopped to check, leaving nothing to chance.

He looked at the camper – all was well. "Since I was already stopped," he told me, "I decided I might as well do a walkaround on the truck." He found the impossible was possible. – there was, indeed, a flat. It was a

Saturday afternoon in rural Tennessee, where there was no place to get the original tire, so he put on the truck's spare tire, and off we went.

We made it to Ashville, where we found ourselves in the middle of various obstacles, including, as Dad put it, "big-time construction" complete with "poor temporary road signs." Somewhere, somehow, he missed a turn, but he thought it was "no prob – I will just to the next exit and find a road going south, which would put us back on track."

It would have worked, too, except the road he chose became a narrow dirt path – "this was crossing Black Mountain (huge mountain, check it out)." Here's what we faced: "VERY big, treacherous (mountain), unpopulated and just a dirt/gravel road going to who knows where."

"I was very anxious about it the whole time," my mom told me.

We toughed it out, though, and eventually found our way back on to the interstate, our destination securely in our targets.

We arrived in the middle of the night, finding a spot "right on the beach (per Mr. Linville Reed's suggestion)" with only one problem: it was the tail end of a very bad storm. "Hard winds," Dad said. "Sand stinging with every step. The pop-up camper was full of sand, the beds included. Everyone was MAD — hot and sweaty with sand in eyes, ears, nose, mouth and butt cracks."

I remember us sitting around with bandanas (probably just extra T-shirts) wrapped around our faces, trying desperately to keep the sand out of our eyes and mouths. I don't recall, however, any special precautions for our butt cracks.

We moved to an inland site the next day, and all returned to normal. For a while.

We headed out to an amusement park, and on the way, another guy alerts us to another flat tire. This time Dad found us with good luck – it was only half flat. He put some air in it, and away we go. We had to stop about four times to air it up, but we finally made it back to the campsite safe and sound.

Now, though, the tire was completely flat, and we had no spare.

"We are just now really starting to have fun," Dad said.

The next day, a neighbor who somehow had a truck like Dad's, let us borrow a spare tire. Dad and my sister Deana headed out to find a place that did repairs, leaving me behind with Mom to play on the beach. I'm really not sure how Deana got saddled with that assignment, but since she's six years older than me, she was probably a lot more help in the flat-tire situation than I would have been. That also holds true today.

Dad and Deana (mostly Dad, I'm sure) got the tires repaired, and they no doubt headed back to the beach full of visions of splashing and playing after having returned as Heroes of the New Tires. Unfortunately, they got delayed.

On the way back to camp, they had a blow-out. Dad put yet another spare on and heads back to the store. "It turns out, the place that originally put my new tires on had damaged my very nice aluminum wheels, causing them to leak," he said. "The tires were actually OK." First of all, let me say that I like the fact that Dad took time to note that they were "very nice" wheels. Again, if you know Doc Hall, you know he likes his vehicles.

He bought a new set of wheels (no word if they were "very nice" or even just "nice"), mounted the tires and head back, once again, for the campsite.

While Dad and Deana were gone, Mom and I had our own adventure at the beach, enjoying a nice stretch of it by ourselves for a bit. And when I say by ourselves, I mean, literally, no one else was in the water. There we were, splashing around, having a big time while watching four or five helicopters flying over us. Mom even pointed them out, and we stood in the water, waving up at the pilots.

After a good day of swimming, we returned to our camper. Along the way, Mom saw something that caught her eye. "I saw the sign up the beach that said no one was allowed in the ocean until further notice because of the sharks," she said. "So much for the beach all by ourselves."

Dad was nonplussed about it. "Deana and I get back to the site only to find out Mom had been trying to feed you to the sharks – oh well, whatever."

Things got back to normal – "VERY boring, ha ha," Dad said – and at the end of the week, it's time to head home. "Get everything loaded and packed and ready to leave," Dad said, "and guess what – flat tire on the camper."

"I was considering just leaving it where it was and getting home," Mom said. "Deana said your dad changed tires more than he changed socks."

So, no wonder it's been almost 30 years since our last beach vacation. Wish us luck. And lots of good tires.

HOLD ON TO TRUE LOVE WHENEVER YOU'RE LUCKY ENOUGH TO FIND IT

by Kevin Hall

He stood next to his car, garden tools loaded in the trunk, a water pail hanging from his hand. The boy, his grandson, about 10, walked out of the house, anxious to tag along, wanting to be a man, wanting to help, wanting to do more than just carry a water bucket while working to stay out of the way.

The old man started to get in the car, hesitated, stepped away.

"I forgot something," he said.

The old man walked back inside, letting the screen door slap shut as the boy stood by. A minute passed, maybe two. The boy peeked through the mesh screen and watched as his grandfather kissed his grandmother, the two of them momentarily acting closer to 18 than 80.

The boy turned away, and soon the old man returned outside.

"I always gotta say goodbye before I go," the old man said.

The two left, off to the garden, off to their lives as the years passed and boy became a teen and the old man became weaker, forgetful. Soon, he stopped eating, as dementia ravaged his mind, making him unable to remember anything, anyone.

But he held on, with occasional glimmers of his old life, recognizing the boy, talking about the garden.

Soon, he could hold on no more. He lived in a hospital bed at the boy's parents' house, while his wife, a tiny woman hobbled by broken bones, lifted by a strong spirit, remained in their house, the bed they shared for more than 60 years.

"Mother, it's time," the boy's father said. "He's slipping, more and more each day. If you don't come now, you'll have waited too late."

Still, she put off.

The plea was repeated, then ignored; repeated, ignored.

Finally, she relented, arriving to see a shadow of her husband.

The old man had been mostly unresponsive for days, his eyes not opening for anything, but as she took his hand, his lids lifted. They sat together, she at the side of his bed, holding his hand, patting it, putting off the only word that remained.

She kissed him, softly. And she said it, "Goodbye."

The old man died the next day.

My grandfather, the old man, would have turned 100 today, and everything I've ever needed to know about love, I learned on those two days.

Some things are worth waiting for.

Some things will never die.

And love – real love, honest love, true love – is a gift.

GRANDFATHERS

by Kevin Hall

My grandfather, with his body's deterioration finally catching up to his mind's head start, stayed bed-bound downstairs while my dad looked after him during the day. It was two generations of Strother Halls, back under one roof, with the younger version now fully in charge, the patriarch at last, helping his Alzheimer's-riddled father ease into this final stage as peacefully as possible.

Those last few months also gave my dad a final peace with his own dad, something he shared with me toward the end of Papa Hall's life.

Dad told me that when he was growing up, the two hadn't been very close, with Dad even wondering if the two men loved each other. I found this shocking since the Papa Hall I knew was about the kindest old grandfather you could ever encounter. My youth at his house was spent hearing tall tales of his youth while we shared glass bottles of Mountain Dew or the occasional Ale-8 (soft drinks that I wasn't allowed to have when at home). We played card games at the kitchen table and read (newspapers for him, Archie comics for me) in our recliners in the living room. We laughed when Granny passed gas, then asked forgiveness by bringing her flowers from the backyard garden.

It couldn't be possible that this man, my grandfather, my Papa Hall, wasn't capable of being anything short of incredible to anyone, let alone his own son, his only son.

But age and grandchildren can change a man, I guess.

I see this every day now with my own dad. Growing up, I knew my dad loved me, but I never knew how much he actually liked me. We weren't close, although we interacted often. When we played catch, I viewed it as a chore; there were no sentimental father/son *Field of Dreams* moments at that time. He seemed miserable to be out there, and I'm sure I was equally unhappy.

What I didn't know then was that his body pretty much stayed in constant pain, the result of back injuries that had taken their toll. Every time he threw a baseball toward me, his body howled with crippling pain, yet he would just grit his teeth and go on because playing catch with your son is just what a man is supposed to do.

Just like my dad realized that his own dad did indeed love him (and that it was a shared feeling), I've come to terms with my own relationship with my dad. Fortunately, we didn't need a deathbed to get to it.

Instead, all it took were grandkids in the form of my sister's three boys.

All three of my nephews think my dad is some sort of superstar, and honestly, I can see why: he is loud and funny, telling tall tales of his youth, sharing soft drinks, playing card games and laughing at Mom when she passes gas. He's become the Papa Hall.

While the two oldest boys, ages 15 and almost 14, still love being around my dad, the youngest, Jon, age 10, worships him. He will call my mom and ask if Dad can come over and play. They are best friends.

Jon recently had a school assignment asking him to write about a hero. He chose Dad (or, Poppa, as the boys call him). Jon wrote that Poppa took them to the Corvette Museum and joined them on a beach trip to North Carolina this summer. Jon told how even though Poppa has had lots of injuries to his hip, leg and back, he has always been there to do things with them and for them. He never gives up. He is a hero.

Yeah, age and grandchildren can change a man. But It can also change a son.

SEWERVILLE: THE LAY OF THE LAND

by Aaron Saylor

Sewardville, Kentucky. A quaint little town, a nice little town, that's what the sign said as you came in on the East Kentucky Parkway. Population eleven thousand, eight hundred and thirty-two people, sixty-four churches, ninety gas stations, and five police officers. Better known as The Mountain, as in, Where you from? I'm from The Mountain.

Out-of-towners snickered about the quaint little nickname, because of course, there really was not a single real mountain anywhere near the south central part of the Bluegrass state. A few high places in the road maybe, knobby ridgetops and hillsides pocked by spindly pines and oaks, but no mountains. The good folks of Sewardville called their hills "mountains," but they weren't mountains and it didn't matter anyway: Morris Mountain, North Fork Mountain, Brown Mountain, Coppers Creek Mountain, all passed for peaks in the great Sewardville mountain chain that really wasn't. So what if they weren't mountains? The people called them mountains. That was all that mattered. The out-of-towners might snicker, the snotty big-city college folk from Lexington or Louisville or points further, but nobody in Sewardville gave a damn because out-of-towners snickered about everything. That was what made them out-of-towners.

In Sewardville, life sung just fine. Just fine, thank you very much. The years drummed along, but the place held tight to its old-fashioned country values. A city ordinance required residents to repaint their houses and mobile homes no less than once every six years. (That ordinance of course didn't apply to brick homes, but then again, there were no brick homes, except for Sewardville mayor Walt Slone's place, and it was outside of the city limits, anyway.) Another ordinance mandated that all lawns be kept trimmed to a height of not more than six inches, with all clippings gathered and bagged for pickup by the sanitation department. Storefronts – though few – were always kept in good order, too, with the owners often seen sweeping their lots, which was pretty easy since there generally weren't many cars in the way.

And the churches of Sewardville! They were so plentiful, and overflowing with the bounties of the Lord! Presbyterian, and Pentecostal, and Baptist, and Southern Baptist, and Emmanuel Baptist, and the Church of God, and the Church of Christ (two of them), and the Church on the Rock, and more, and more, and more. So many more. So many churches. There was even a Catholic Church. Oh my! And oh my! There was even a synagogue, for the one Jewish family in town! Actually that was their garage but nobody quibbled about it because it was important that Sewardville be respected for its compassion towards all.

The people filed into their church of choice every Sunday as expected, and twice on Easter and Christmas. Bright, grinning, dressed and pressed. They shook hands with their preachers, called for additions to their prayer lists, tithed the required ten percent of their gross income as supported by the W2 forms that were given to the church elders every year. They drew on their vast wells of empathy and made little signs for the community's yards that said PRAYER IN, DRUGS OUT and GOD CAN HELP YOU and JESUS IS COMING, GET READY. They stood in their pews and sang songs for the Lord and for each other. They wrapped their arms around their neighbors and promised to keep the darkness away forever.

There was more to Sewardville than churches, of course. It wasn't the churches, but the *people* in the churches that made Sewardville. Strong people, they were – the kind of people who stood for something. For God, for the stars and stripes, for the Ten Commandments, and, most importantly on this Earth, for their families. And what beautiful families they had – happy children, with bright eyes, tousled hair and big dreams. The schools of Sewardville were filled with dreams, and one day the dreamers of those dreams would bring their glory home. Every year at graduation, the guest speaker said that. One day the dreams would all come true, they just knew that one of these days, the dreams *had* to come true. Even as the years passed, and no dreamer returned, parents kept telling their children that it was going to happen. Maybe *they* could be the one to do it.

A particular flower grew free in the soft hills of Seward County… and nowhere else in the world. Not one single other place. An issue of

National Geographic verified this in 1914. *Orchistradae Mountain* – the Mountain orchid, whose long white petals drooped downward and came together at the ends like tiny hands clasped in prayer.

There was more, of course. More to Sewardville than churches, and children, and flowers.

There was always more.

Sewardville had its dark corners, too. It's only fair that these dark corners must be noted. Folks who lived in Sewardville called their town the Mountain, but knew just the same that the Kentucky State Police had a different name for their town, one not so quaint and not so nice.

The boys in gray uniforms called it Sewerville. So did the Federal Bureau of Investigation, the *Lexington Herald-Leader*, the Bureau of Alcohol, Tobacco, and Firearms, the Governor's Task Force for Drug Prevention, the *Louisville Courier-Journal,* the American Civil Liberties Union, the Cabinet for Health and Human Resources, the Educate America First! campaign, the *New York Times, Newsweek,* and the university dental students who came around in their RV's once a year to clean teeth and pull cavities free of charge. Once even, a reporter from *60 Minutes* came to town and referred to the place as Sewerville, but fortunately Sheriff Slone was there to bust up the camera before that made it to the national audience.

WTVL-TV out of Lexington kept a news van open and a reporter on call at all times, just in case something newsworthy happened in Sewardville. Of course, something usually did. Sometimes it was big news – one night a murder, one night a bank robbery, one night some kid overdoses on pain pills, one night a meth lab explodes and kills an old lady and her three grandchildren. Sometimes it was not such big news – a stray dog problem, a dead cow by the Kwik Mart, some parent got worked up because the teacher told her kid to shut his smart mouth. Whatever. Whatever. But no matter how large or small the news story, WTVL stood at the ready, beaming every last scrap of Sewardville drama out over the Eastern half of the state. They usually sent that Carla Haney girl to report. She came off like a snot, that's what Boone Sumner always said. She was always just *so* quick to put the worst face of Sewardville up so the public could see it, like that was the only face that Sewardville possessed.

Oh yes, Sewerville – Sewardville – had its dark corners, and these dark corners must be noted, in the spirit of true Christian honesty. Boone Sumner tells the story about how one time, in Sewardville, a couple of fat lawyers from Cincinnati went hiking, out around Furnace Road, on the back side of Brown Mountain, just past where Highway 220 passes over Coppers Creek. Folks familiar with that particular part of the woods know that there aren't many good reasons for hiking out around that part of the Mountain. Fat lawyers from Cincinnati know it now, too; a couple of their fat buddies came across a marijuana field and stepped on some dynamite caps. The two unfortunate barristers got shipped home in black vinyl bags, some rather unfortunate assembly required to get their bodies in enough shape for a funeral. You can ask Boone – he'll tell you.

(Boone Sumner is really a nice guy, he gets a bad rap around the Mountain sometimes because of the company he keeps, but he's a nice guy and you can count on him to give the straight story. Now, what was he doing wondering around a marijuana field shortly after these two lawyers got dynamited? Well, you can ask him that, too. Maybe some people just have a knack for being in the wrong place at the wrong time.)

Another time in Sewardville, this twenty-one year old badhair named Jesse Johnson got busted by the F.B.I. for running a grand theft auto ring. He stole diesel rigs and tractor trailers from rest stop parking lots all along the East Kentucky Parkway, ten wheelers up to eighteen wheelers. If the driver was asleep inside, Jesse just took that driver down the road a mile or so and kick him out in the ditch line. Then, he ran the trucks under cover of his co-conspirators until the trucks ended up in West Virginia or Michigan or maybe even NEW YORK CITY, and a few thousand dollars ended up in Jesse's pocket.

Once, Jesse Johnson even tried to run a heisted big rig all the way to Thunder Bay. That's Thunder Bay, Canada. In those days, though, it was hard to drive a stolen eighteen-wheeled flatbed tractor trailer across an international border, especially when the license plate hadn't even been changed (even if it *was* "just Canada"), and the F.B.I. quickly impounded the truck and tossed poor Jesse in the hoosegow. He broke out, of course. You know he'd be one to bust out. Even better, he broke *in* to the F.B.I. impoundment lot, and stole his truck back. *He stole his truck back from the F.B.I.* Then he drove that eighteen-wheeled flatbed tractor trailer all the way up the Mountain, took it to his Uncle Roy's property, dug a big hole - a BIG DAMN HOLE – and buried the motherfucker. Buried it. Right in the ground. An eighteen-wheeled flatbed tractor trailer. Swear to God.

This other time in Sewardville, a sheriff's deputy got arrested for running a prostitution ring from the confines of his police cruiser. Seems somebody saw a twelve year-old girl get in the backseat with an older gentleman. Nobody would've thought anything about it, except the old man was a deacon at the Presbyterian Church and the little girl was a Baptist preacher's granddaughter. Baptists and Presbyterians just don't mix.

A different time in Sewardville, a seventeen-year-old kid was arrested for drinking a Budweiser in public. The cops also found him tossing firecrackers at his neighbor from the front porch of the mobile home the kid shared with his grandmother and two aunts. When the police searched that mobile home they found three hundred and forty-two fully automatic Russian-made assault rifles, ninety-six hand grenades, twenty pounds of C-4 plastic explosive, eight samurai swords, five Kevlar bulletproof vests, six fifty-caliber Desert Eagle handguns, and a bazooka. A GODDAMN BAZOOKA, as the investigating officers later referred to that particular piece of weaponry. The grandmother defended the kid's innocence; she kicked a state trooper in the balls and pushed another one off the porch before they finally got her under control. Her grandson ended up with a whopping eight months in juvie. When he got out, he came home and burned the trailer down. Granny was still inside. Whoops.

Same kid went back to the pokey for that unfortunate homicide slash arson incident, sentenced to life. Damn lucky he didn't get lined up for the gas chamber He escaped, of course. (People from Sewardville aren't too big on jail.) He and one of his pokey buddies hid in the trash one night, rode out in a garbage truck the next morning. There was a two-day manhunt across the state for these gentlemen. Lead story on the nightly news both days.

The pair turned up, of course. Know what happens to jailbirds when they ride out of jail in the morning garbage? They learn a little lesson about trash compactors. A day after they disappeared, these two turned up at the city landfill. Mostly, they turned up.

The youngest Death Row inmate in American history hailed from Sewardville. This kid was all of sixteen years old when he broke into his neighbor's house and sliced up a three year old little girl and then chased her mother down in the backyard and carved her up, too. Awful. What a sick fuck. The good people of Sewardville stopped talking about him years ago – just too awful, just too sick. But if you know who to ask, someone might tell you that Walt Slone still carries a standing offer of ten thousand dollars to any man that guts the little shit, because Walt went to high school with the little girl's daddy and they played on the same basketball team.

In the early 1900's, a passenger train route went right through the middle of Sewardville. The town was widely held as a thriving industrial and cultural center of Appalachia.

In 2009, only fourteen percent of Sewardville households had a car that was less than 5 years old.

If you are ever in Sewardville and you happen to read the obituary section of the local weekly newspaper, and there you see a young lady or gentleman taken from this world well before their time, you are forgiven if your mind wanders. If there is no cause of death listed in the obituary, you can chalk that one up to the pills. People just don't like to read that anymore, so the good folks at the Sewardville *Times* just leave it out as a community service.

One morning, a young morphine addict dropped dead on the steps of Sewardville Elementary School. Right off the bus – she was a student there. Third grade.

The truth is, in Sewardville, it's not too difficult to get those precious pills. If there's one thing people in Sewardville know, it's how to get pills.

At the local free health clinic, a guy showed up, begging for a new 'scrip for pain medicine. Not that he was sick, or in any real pain, he just wanted some pills. He loved pills. Any kind of pills. Just give me some pills. The doctor said no, the man yelled at him, the doctor still said no. After a short while this discussion got heated, and the triage nurse called the Sewardville sheriff's department for back-up. Sheriff Slone himself showed up half an hour later. Five minutes before he got there, the man who loved pills lost his fucking mind, took out a .38 snub-nose, and shot the doctor in the face.

Seven drug-related murders occurred in Sewardville in the past year, along with eighteen rapes, ninety-one armed robberies, and three kidnappings. Sheriff Slone and his six deputies cover the county, and two roving state troopers help out as needed. The town of Sewardville itself has no proper police department.

Five or six times a year, somebody breaks into the Sewardville Rx and takes whatever they damn well please. Once, a high school cheerleader named Wanda busted up the pharmacy, stole every Hydrocodone and Percoset in the place, then crushed up and snorted them right there on the pharmacy floor. The police determined that this was Wanda's definitive course of action because after she snorted all those pills, poor Wanda passed out within fifteen minutes and died in under thirty. Right there, next to the condom rack. Sheriff Slone came down to look at the body. "Nice tits," he said. Then he went to the drive-in movie theater and fucked Wanda's sister.

The public school system employs more people than any private business in Sewardville. Yet, 34% of Sewardvillians drop out before high school graduation.

The number two employer in Sewardville is Regency Manufacturing, the only factory in town, where workers reupholstered second-hand couches for $7.00 an hour.

Sewardville's number three employer? The department of sanitation.

More?

There was always more.

But every place had problems, every little town and big city in America. There was no point in dwelling on the problems. Better to talk about the good things – the children, the good church people, the family values, the solid bedrock strength of the community. Sewardville was a place where people stood up and sang in church. Sewardville was where children laughed in the city park. In Sewardville, grandfathers took their grandsons fishing, and grandmothers taught their granddaughters how to make yellow cakes and perfect white icings. In Sewardville, mothers and fathers and brothers and sisters and sons and daughters and aunts and uncles and pretty much everyone in town wrapped their arms around each other and promised to keep the darkness of the world away forever.

Sewardville, Kentucky. Population eleven thousand, eight hundred and thirty-two people, sixty-four churches, ninety gas stations, and five police officers. The good folks called their town the Mountain, as in, Where you from? I'm from The Mountain. Sure, there was no mountain, no mountain at all. Just a few hills. But somewhere along the line, people saw mountains on T.V. or maybe even read about them in books, and they decided they ought to have a mountain of their own, an honest-to-god mountain, right there in the stubby foothills of Appalachia. So they gave themselves one.

NONSENSE

by Kevin Hall

<u>one.</u>

She smelled familiar.

It hit me, or rather, quite literally, my nose, while sitting in a movie theater, sharing a box of Sour Patch Kids. She didn't like the green ones. Or maybe it was yellow. One of them, even though I'm not sure I can tell a difference; to me, they all taste like sour, if that's even a flavor. Probably not, I guess.

We'd been hanging out for a few weeks by then, spending as much of our days together as possible. Same with our evenings. I held out hope for our nights. Until then, though, the hours of 8 a.m. to 10 p.m. (maybe midnights on the weekends, if lucky) would suffice, the non-date dates ending with high-five or a fist bump, anything for physical contact, desperate as that might seem. Some nights, when caution found itself out of mind/out of sight, we'd shake hands, the unspoken agreement being that our hands could linger a bit longer than necessary, our fingers anxiously feeling out for each other, grasping for signs that the other was just as nervous (or, hopefully, excited).

But at least we were together, which is the primary part of the dating battle — finding someone you can somehow convince to do something with you somewhere at sometime. She enjoyed spending time with me, and I with her, so the "someone" part proved relatively easy. The trickier subjects were the other "somes."

It should have been easy, and under other circumstances, well, I guess it would have been, but it's never been that way for me. There's always a catch, always a caveat, always a fine print. For her, it was me. Or, more accurately, it was my ex-wife. Actually, it wasn't the ex-wife so much as it was the fact that I had an ex-wife, one, I might add, whom I had only been divorced from for a matter of weeks.

I didn't want a girlfriend. Girlfriends only lead to fiancées, which only lead to wives, which only lead to ex-wives. I tried that route. Didn't like it. Instead, I wanted companionship, and that she provided.

"She" was Maria.

Sigh.

Only I didn't know that at the time. What I knew then was that we were two people fast becoming best friends who kept finding ways to make our schedules intertwine, finding excuses to visit each other, finding ourselves running out of reasons and no longer caring.

She was my girlfriend. I just didn't know it. Hell, I didn't even know I liked her.

She knew, though.

She just didn't tell me, figuring I'd eventually figure it out on my own.

What she didn't know, however, is that I'm a slow learner.

This should have been abundantly obvious, it would seem, as we sat in the theater, waiting for the previews to start prior to a discounted mid-day showing of *Peter Pan*. Instead of worrying about important matters, like finding clever ways to touch her hand, which could, should God decide to smile upon me that day, lead to small bouts of intense hand-holding, I obsessed over trivial matters, mainly the origin of her odor.

I shouldn't say "odor" because that implies stinkiness, which she most certainly was not. She smelled sweet, almost a bit chocolaty. In fact …

"You smell like cookies," I told her.

She turned her head, cocking it almost imperceptibly to the side, trying to figure out an appropriate response. I doubt there's a predetermined Mars/Venus retort for that one.

"No, really, you smell like cookies."

She laughed, the best of the true reactions, the moment when you're the most honest with yourself and just share the joy of the moment with someone else.

"I think, maybe, that it's my lotion," she told me.

I considered this, weighing the potential impact such a discovery could have on our relationship, despite one of us not admitting that's what this was and the other waiting for the first to come around. Mere lotion, store-bought in some large chain or specialty boutique, could in no way be responsible for this scent, this capturing of her essence, her entire being encapsulated by one whiff of sweet goodness. I refused to believe it came at price.

"No, I think cookie is just your natural smell."

She smiled and nestled in beside me, the first open recognition of some sort of feelings of attraction toward me. We didn't hold hands, but our legs touched some, and that was enough for the time. Let's not rush things. Slow and steady. We had forever. We just didn't know it.

And to think it all might have started simply because I have a bit of a sweet tooth.

two.

I held the tiny flip-flop in my hand like a talisman, unconsciously fingering its words. It reminded me of her, a careful message ("I ♥ Robert"), self-serving to those not in on the joke.

It kept me close to her, kept her near, even as night fell and she remained somewhere else. Miles away or across the street, it didn't really matter. She was gone.

Not permanently, of course. That would come later, although we didn't know it then, not that we would have believed it anyhow. We had our rhythms. We had our inside jokes, our secret codes, our private moments.

We had us.

What we hadn't had, though, was sex.

Oh, we'd had opportunities, of course, but something would always crop up, usually some sort of emotional meltdown rendering us unfit to continue. We wanted it to be perfect. I think, on some levels, we needed it to be perfect. We pictured ourselves a storybook romance.

Sometimes, though, we couldn't find the words.

Often, she'd just get scared, telling me she knew I'd leave her, that I'd be the one to break her heart, even though we both knew, deep down, it would always be the other way around. So she put up a wall, telling me from time to time that we were finished, that she could never be with me, that she didn't want me.

I knew she didn't mean it.

I usually blamed it on something else.

And she knew she usually didn't mean it.

She almost always blamed it on something else.

So maybe we weren't perfect, but really, who is? What we had was good enough for us, whatever that was.

Tonight, though, she was gone, off to New Orleans, something to do with work, some sort of award or training or maybe neither. Maybe it was just Mardi Gras.

I had showered, thinking I'd go to bed early, telling myself it was to rest up for work, knowing it was because sleeping was the only thing that helped pass the time while she was gone.

I sat on my love seat, about 10 o'clock, in my robe, reading my Dickens, when she called. Friendly greetings exchanged, brief recaps of the day, the usual banter.

A couple of minutes later, my doorbell rang.

I sprang from my seat, making my way into the kitchen, crouching behind a cabinet.

"Someone is at my door," I told her, trying hard not to freak out and failing miserably.

"Well, who is it?"

"I don't know."

"Aren't you gonna look?

"No. It can't be good. It's late." Plus, and there was no real reason to tell her this, I was scared.

"Maybe you should at least peek out."

"Are you outside?"

"No."

"Then I'm not answering the door."

"Just go look."

So I did.

And there she was.

"You're supposed to be in New Orleans."

"You're supposed to kiss me, but I'll settle for a hug."

She scooted forward and hugged me before taking a seat on the couch. I sat across from her on the ottoman.

She smiled, said, "I brushed my teeth after the flight, just so you know. I mean, you don't have to worry about that."

I finally took the hint.

"I'm glad you're back."

"Me, too."

"I've missed you."

"Me, too."

"Would it kill you to just say you've missed me?"

"You know I don't work that way, responding to pressured situations to say what you think I ought to say."

"I just want to know you want me."

Silence.

"See," I told her, pulling away. "Well, I'm here whenever you want me … you just don't want me."

"I never said that."

"Yes you have. You actually said those exact words – 'I don't want to be with you.'"

She straddled me on the ottoman. "I don't know why I'm doing this then since I don't want to be with you." She kissed me, with intent.

"Are you sure you want this to happen?" I asked.

She answered by taking my hand, walking with me to my bed.

Finally, after eight months, it happened.

Eight months of wooing.

Eight months of trying.

Eight months of waiting.

And, honestly, eight months of fantasizing.

She was beneath me.

She finished first, except she's not finished.

Another.

And another.

I chugged toward mine, knowing it's going to be huge, feeling it in all parts of my body, all parts of my being.

I couldn't wait anymore. It was at the point of happening, and just when the feeling was about to overtake me …

"I love you," she told me.

… we misfired on our movements, and I ended up outside of her.

I tried to scramble the best I can, grabbing hold of myself, trying to get back in.

But it was too late.

So there I was, after all this time, finally having sex with the girl of my dreams, and I still just got off holding my own dick.

It wasn't perfect, I guess, but maybe it didn't have to be anyone else's storybook.

"I love you, too," I told her, absentmindedly tracing a shape on her back.

I think it was a tiny footprint.

three.

I'd never seen a sadder birthday girl.

She smiled maybe once, earlier, between sushi and cheesecake, but it was less of a smile and more of the memory of an inside joke once forgotten before slipping back into her own thoughts. She waved at me from the far end of the table. I don't think she knew who I was.

There were songs, the standard birthday choruses, of course, mixed with some Bocephus and Beatles and, oddly enough, "Come On, Eileen." She had a candle and blew it out, her wish lasting about as long as the drifting smoke. If she even made one. She never told us, we didn't ask.

Pianos played behind her, begging her to dance, just one twist of the hips, one shake of the ass, in her sleeveless black top and jeans that every man noticed but none dared approach. No one wants to dance at someone else's party, I guess.

Until they did. The dancing, I mean. And singing. Stories shared as beer slopped from clumsily poured pitchers, more focus paid to laughs than a steady hand.

" … they have me down for working Saturday, but I'm pretty sure I'm going to call in sick and go meet Misty instead. Her profile looked soooooo hot, dude …"

"… saw Aerosmith three times. Knew most of the words to everything, too. Particularly that one they did with Run DMC, you know, 'Walk This …"

"… 'we went back inside, sat down, had a few drinks, and all we kept talking about, was' …"

Not her.

Not one word.

She left the table, slipping through the crowd, left or right, you couldn't really tell, the heads and bodies blending into a mass of perfect hair cuts and white smiles, at least until the drunk sweats took over.

She was gone. To smoke, I guess. Or maybe just to feel the cold lick her skin, the February wind reminding of her of reality, bitter and distant.

Twenty-nine years old, but not a day past high school. Couldn't leave it behind, or maybe it just followed her, no matter how hard she tried to shake it off, a dog coming in from the rain. Maybe a few pills, sure. Some drinks. Whatever it takes, you know.

Yeah, just a dog coming in from a cold rain.

I left to find her, no shining armor, just a blazer and jeans. She stood alone, huddled against the bricks, warm smoke in her lungs and cold breath out her mouth. She hugged one arm across her body, fighting for heat while the other hand held tight to the cigarette. I gave her my blazer.

"You'll freeze," she told me.

"You'll have to smoke fast, then."

She inhaled, blew it out the side of her mouth, careful to keep it out of my face.

"You look too smart to smoke," she said.

"I probably also look too smart to stand outside in the snow, and, well, here I am."

She moved toward me, turning a shoulder near my chest. I took the hint, put my arms around her, pulling her in close, smelling the smoke in her hair.

"You having a good birthday?" I asked.

She looked away, answered, "Yeah."

"I don't believe you."

"It's cold out here."

"I know it is. I'm the one without a jacket." I leaned to her ear, whispered, "And you're the one avoiding my question."

She moved back a half step, still keeping the embrace. "I answered."

"You lied."

"I have to pee. Walk me to the bathroom."

"And you'll have fun after?"

She turned away, grabbing my hand as we walked back inside, the doormen checking our hands and letting us pass. We weaved through the people, her arm reaching back, keeping a close grip on my fingers, guiding me darker and darker, away from the music, anywhere but here.

I saw the bathroom signs, promised to wait for her but only if she gave back my jacket. "We should be so lucky to see those shoulders, my dear." A fair trade, and then she disappeared through the door while I waited longer than I should have.

four.

I woke up to the sound of her crying, alone, in a pool of her own vomit.

Not really crying, either. More like an animal, wounded, frightened, howling in the middle of the night until someone, something, else comes along.

She couldn't stand, not yet, not for a few hours. Her friends had left, off for more drinks in another house, somewhere far from her, miles away from her misery.

I picked her up, carried her to the bedroom.

"I deserve better than this," she said, her words slurred and slow.

"I think you have that mixed around," I told her.

"Yeah … yeah, you got it. You, yeah, that's it. You deserve better than this."

She kissed me on the ear, smelling a bit like potato chips, a lot like vodka, but mostly like puke.

"You take good care of me."

"Yeah, well, you're my girl."

She lunged for my mouth, her lips dry and open. Her tongue left her mouth, beginning its probe inches in front of my face. I put my hands on her shoulders, kept her in place.

"Not right now, babe. OK?"

She nodded, the last nod being too much, her head remaining down, her chin seemingly stuck to her chest.

I sat her down on the bed, turned to get a washcloth from the bathroom. She slumped back, her body limp, all but lifeless.

I took my time drawing the warm water, wondering how long this would last. The night, the sickness, the us. I think we both knew. It's probably why she couldn't sit up, why I couldn't let go.

She started snoring, shallow bursts, a brief exhalation. One hand went behind her head, played with her hair, lightly touching her scalp. I wiped off her mouth, rinsed her face. She felt warm.

Back to the bathroom for a toothbrush, thinking no one deserved to go to sleep with that on their breath. I couldn't find hers, leaving two options, well, three if you count "let her go to sleep with vomit breath" as an option, which I did not. I could rinse her mouth with toothpaste and the washcloth, or I could use my brush.

She was my girl.

I used my brush.

Gently in her mouth, I rubbed her teeth and gums, sliding it across her tongue, trying to make her feel fresh again, like the girl from the evening. The music. The food. The laughter with friends. She was herself again, for once, the her from the movie theatre long ago, the her I fell for, the her of my dreams.

Then came the nightmare.

There's always a nightmare these days.

She woke up, tried to talk but mostly gagged on the toothbrush. Her eyes watered before she focused them, seeing it was me, realizing what I was doing. I stopped cleaning.

"I want you to leave me in the morning," she whispered.

"I can't do that."

She started taking her shirt off, struggling to get it over her head.

"I need you to leave me. Let me be alone."

"You can't be alone."

She sat there, nude on top. I'm not sure what had happened to her bra. I'm not going to ask about where it went while I was asleep.

There could be good explanation.

Some things are best left to the unknown.

She took my hand, cupped it to her left breast.

"Leave me."

"You have a funny way of saying goodbye."

The tears started.

The whispers left.

"I fucking hate you. I want you to get out of my life."

She could be loud when she drank. She didn't know what she wanted, letting the alcohol talk.

I hugged her, pulling her face into my neck.

"It's OK, baby. Nothing's going to hurt you now."

She yelled again. I'm not sure what she said. It was mostly a mix of cursing and slurring, some sobs mixed in. I looked at her. She shut her eyes, kept them closed.

I helped her back on the bed, wanting her to rest, thinking sleep would make this end faster, bring tomorrow quicker.

I held her, whispered to her, doing anything possible to help her sleep.

She babbled.

"I want you to leave me tomorrow."
"I want you to stay with me forever."
"You deserve better than this."
"I deserve better than this."

I'd heard it before. I learned to ignore it. I kept holding her until we're both asleep.

About an hour later, I wake up as she's leaving the bed.

"Where are you going?"

"I have to go to the bathroom."

And off she goes, in search of the toilet. A few minutes pass; she's not back. I get up to check on her, see her shirt through the crack in the door. She's crawling back to the room. I go to bring her back.

She wasn't crawling.

She had collapsed outside the room, a few feet from the door. She had pissed herself, was sitting there crying.

"Maria, did you piss on the floor?

"No, I didn't."

"Well, I have wet shorts, panties and a big stain on the carpet that suggest otherwise."

"I didn't. I promise."

I picked her up, sat her on the edge of the bed. Took off her shorts and panties, replacing them with a pair of my boxers. I got her back in bed, wrapped myself around her, her body covered by mine.

"Nothing's gonna harm you, not while I'm around," I whispered. She finally smiled; she loved *Sweeney Todd*.

She fell asleep, snoring her soft breaths.

I wonder what her dreams were.

I didn't have any.

I stayed awake.

I wondered what happened next.

five.

The ending, when it came, tasted bittersweet.

Moments came and passed, like summer weather, sunny and warm, thunder and floods. The good washed away by the bad, the bad drowned out by the good.

We must have been in a drought on this day.

I'm an open book, and now I see maybe I should have been more closed off, particularly when it came to things involving her, but since everything was a thing involving her, I wouldn't have had anything to write or talk about. So talk I did, or, as happened on more than one occasion, write I did.

A couple of weeks earlier, I had written a column about how the Internet can make breaking up different these days, as social sites like MySpace and Facebook seem to gain some sort of digital satisfaction out of posting the latest bad news from your personal life. Personally, I enjoyed what I had to say, but I guess that's pretty much the case with most everything I write, particularly columns. I mean, if I didn't like a column, which is just my opinion on matters of importance to me, who will? That's not egotistical; that's just basic writing.

Apparently, a few others liked it, too, with some taking the time to put pen to paper (or, more accurately, finger to keypad) to write comments on our Web site. One wrote about how people in a break-up need to realize there are other people out there to meet and date. Another guy, a male mind you, suggested we go out one evening and hang out as a way to get my mind off my ex.

Well, clearly there are two problems there, the first being that I guess these letters weren't really supporting the theories posited in my column but were instead trying to cheer up my heartache, and that's the second, and bigger, problem: there was no heartache. I'm not single. I'm not going through a break-up. So if these people are confused and think I'm suddenly single, then that means …

Shit. Maria is going to think I overstated our personal life again.

I guess I had it coming ("We all got it coming, kid," Clint Eastwood says in *Unforgiven*, and damn, I guess the ol' cowboy nailed that piece of philosophy).

"How could you?" she asked, her voice sounding amazingly calm I now realize given the level of Armageddon she was about to verbally unleash over the telephone.

"How could I what?"

"Don't play stupid with me."

I wasn't playing stupid. Stupid is a serious way of life for me with her. I had no idea what she was talking about, causing me to ask what was going on.

Stupid me.

"Your column. In the paper."

"Oh, that. Don't worry about it. Our circulation is so small, I mean, really, no one will read it."

"And it's online."

"Nobody reads that either."

"There are already comments."

"OK, let's just assume people have read it," I told her, having great difficulty hiding my excitement over the quick response from readers.

"You have no business telling my business."

"It's my business. The column is about me."

"Well of course it is. You're the most self-involved person I've ever met."

I would have had a difficult time arguing that statement had she even given me the chance.

"I just can't believe you'd write those things about going out with other people," she continued. "Do you just not ever consider anyone else's feelings?"

I pointed out that I hadn't actually written the stuff about going out with other people, a fact I thought truly wrapped up the argument for me but one she readily overlooked. I tried to state my well-reasoned argument: "Any reasonable moron could see what's happening here."

I really should have thought that one out more.

"So I'm a 'reasonable moron'?"

"No no no. You're not being reasonable at all."

I guess at this point I'd lost all interest in civility. Oddly enough, she hadn't.

"Look, just consider my feelings when you say these things, or write them, or whatever," she told me, somehow turning almost calm, almost normal.

Almost.

And I'm really to blame for the failure to drop the "almost."

"Well, I'll try to keep that in mind," I answered, "but if you're going to continue reading my work, I wish you'd consider comprehending it, since really, that's the most important part of reading."

I waited for her response, but none came. I kept the attack going.

"Besides, the column is about me, not you, and I wish you'd figure that out, preferably more on the sooner side rather than the later."

"No, your column is about how you want to show everyone how smart you are and for you to be able to say how great you are."

"Now how do you figure that?"

"All you ever write about is yourself and talking about books you read and movies you watch and 'Boy, I'm so smart.'"

"Well, keeping in mind that the only book I really remember writing about is Harry Potter, I sincerely doubt I have ever tried to allude to my intelligence, particularly using children's literature as Exhibit A. And besides, if reading a book is your idea of what makes a person smart, then that really says a whole lot about you as a person."

She hung up.

I smelled blood and wanted more. I called back.

Wasting no time to allow me to begin critical statements on her behalf, she immediately launched into one of her patented "you think you're so smart" rants, which mainly come out when her own insecurities have her feeling stupid. And by "insecurities," I mean "my harsh comments."

But I wasn't putting up with it this night — "Just because you have no discernible talent, don't disparage someone who does."

"I can't stand you," she yelled. "I'm miserable with you."

"Well then allow me to get out of your life so I'm not holding you back. I'm sure once I'm gone, you're life will be able to flourish out of its current level of mediocrity and you can go on to achieve all your dreams. You can finally be an actress and can quit talking about it and just do it. You know, because clearly your lack of a career in that profession has more to do with me than it does with the fact that you haven't fucking acted since the third fucking grade."

So, as you can see, we had a good night.

I let go.

She let go.

Over. It was over.

Finally.

I guess that's the way the cookie crumbles.

ANALYZE THIS: A PROMISE CAN BE A PAIN IN THE ASS

by Kevin Hall

A friend has found herself in a bit of a conundrum.

You see, a little more than a year ago, she started dating this guy, and as often is the case in new romances, she found herself fancying this fellow, wanting to do whatever it takes to make him happy.

Foolish girl.

She told her boyfriend that if they stayed together a year, they could forego the traditional route of celebrating their first anniversary with paper. Instead, she agreed to treat him to a night of anal passion. (I'm curious as to if their 50th anniversary, traditionally the "golden" anniversary" will be complete with a night of urinating on each other).

At first, the girl thought it was an unlikely achievement, being doubtful a relationship would last a year. However, for many guys, the mere possibility of ass sex will cause them to be on their best behavior for an indefinite period of time.

(Personal note: Although I've never experimented with butt play and cannot speak from experience, I must say the thought of it is not the least bit appealing. To each their own, I guess).

Fast forward 12 months and change – the couple is still together, yet her anal promise so far rings hollow. The girl is now backing down from her agreement, which is posing problems in the relationship, primarily because the boyfriend keeps bringing it up, pretty much just demanding that they follow through with it.

Compounding the problem is that the boy, in his 20s, was a virgin when they met, something my friend couldn't claim. Well, vaginally speaking, of course – she has never had anal sex, which was part of the reason she promised him the ass.

And now the guy is holding on to that promise, saying it would be "something special" between the two of them. She says their regular sex is special, but she just clearly doesn't understand the thinking of the human male. Most guys, if not all, want to be the first at something with their girlfriend. Vagina virginity gone? They'll take the ass. Ass cherry gone? Look out, armpit.

Why is this? It's all part of a historical perspective. Men want to be remembered. We all recall that Neil Armstrong was the first to walk on the moon. Who was the second? Who cares? (For the record, it was Buzz Aldrin).

So what can she do to get out of this?

She's tried explaining that she's quite certain it will hurt. (An aside: A comedian once said he's afraid of having anal sex with his girlfriend because he's afraid he'll hurt her. And he's even more afraid that he won't. You just don't want a girl saying, "Mmm, that's comfortable."). The boyfriend won't listen, though. It's been suggested that she just tell him to punch her in the face, since that, too, will hurt, but without the indignity of using her ass as an entry point.

So far, though, he won't budge, and if you have any suggestions on how to get out of this, please send them my way, and I'll pass them on to her. As it now stands, it looks like she's might just have to bend over and, literally, take it like a man.

That's unfortunate for her, but the ultimate moral of the story, boys and girls, is this: Don't let your mouth write a check that your ass can't cash.

THE SWEET SMELL OF PINE NEEDLES

By Aaron Saylor

The bar's closing. Is it really that late?

Damn. Elizabeth won't like this. She sends me to the bar so she can have some time to herself, but the bar sends me right back to her. Third night this week I've been here. It's not my favorite place in the world but I seem to end up here a lot. This time, I've only been here for seven hours; when she kicked me out today, I got the impression that this time, she was thinking more in terms of years. Elizabeth, Elizabeth, my Elizabeth

The clean smell of gin rises from underneath my collar, a pleasant smell, like pine needles – so sweet, now, in the summertime! Gin smells like pine needles, that's what Dad used to say and the older I get and the more gin I drink and the more I realize Dad was so right. I only drink the good stuff, the Bombay Sapphire. That bottle looks so pretty and bright blue up there on the shelf, beaming at you, waiting for you, saying *kiss me kiss me kiss me*. Some people say it's all the same going down – poison is poison, no matter how pretty it is or how sweet it smells like pine needles – but let me tell you, no. Bombay Sapphire smells like the very best pine needles, what a good blue gin and tonight I have drunk quite a lot of good blue gin that smells like the best pine needles and so now I smell like pine needles, too.

But Elizabeth does not like pine needles. I can't tell you why, but she doesn't. I would think she would enjoy a good whiff of pine needles better than anybody. She's gotten her share over the years, God knows. On my collar, on my breath, on my coat, in the carpet where I puked and she had to clean up after me.

I want another drink. Is it really too much to ask for just one more drink before this shitty bar closes? What a dump. Dark. Unclean. I hear water dripping behind the walls no really I swear I do. Why the hell do I hang out here? The glasses on the bar look like they need to be washed again. These old wooden stools look like dangerous rickety. I remember when they were new. They felt almost comfortable back in those days. A man could sit on one and not feel like he'd get thrown in the floor if he leaned too far in one direction.

Now they need some paint. Maybe some fresh leather padding. Maybe just a new cushion, something in a happier color, purple maybe. Royal Purple like a king's crown, not purplish black like a bruise.

I raise my hand to get the bartender's attention, and notice he's already staring at me. I know what that stare means, don't think I don't know what that stare means. He thinks I'm drunk. Of course, I *am* drunk. But he thinks I'm *too* drunk, that I'm one of those guys that gets his tab and then wads it up and throws it back and maybe takes a haymaker swing at the bartender for good measure. But, the thing is, I'm clearly not one of those guys. Those guys don't wear thousand-dollar suits or diamond-studded Rolexes and don't have laminated business cards that say *Northeastern Bank Vice President, Mortgage Division*, either. No, I'm one of the good guys in this world. And frankly, I don't need those looks from that bartender. What an asshole. Who does he think he is? I come in here a lot; he doesn't need to look at me that way. There's nothing wrong with me. I may be drunk but I'm not an idiot. That bartender *wishes* he could find something wrong with me. He wants to cut me off. He wants a reason to get tough with me, to raise his voice and show the bar who's boss. Fuck him. I got money. I pay my tab in this town. I pay a lot of tabs in this town. What's he worried about? Fuck him. He's a bartender, not a babysitter. I'm not a baby here. Asshole.

I raise my hand again, stretch a little higher. I'm a polite drunk. "Hey, man," I say to the asshole. "Can I have another drink, please?" So polite, so civilized, so in control of myself. People ought to be more civilized in this world. I bet none of the other jerks in here are civilized as me.

"Sorry, Gary, you just had last call," says the asshole. "Ready for your tab?"

"Just one more, please," I say.

I wonder why I come here. This clown at the bar doesn't even know who I am he must be new. I should find a new bar. A new bar that appreciates its paying customers. Fuck him. Fuck this bar.

I wonder why I come here.

Pine needles.

Elizabeth.

I met Elizabeth in a Lexington bookstore, a gigantic two-story place called Russo's that had thick maroon carpeting and more books in it than the public libraries of most small American cities. We were both seniors in college. Elizabeth worked at Russo's as a cashier, with a deep love for 18th and 19th century Gothic literature. She was fascinated by novels and poems that I never knew existed, written by authors whose names I'd never heard before she whispered them to me.

My literary tastes, on the other hand, tended to fall into a more contemporary vein: I didn't really like books. People like me, we don't have time for books. But, the hot word around campus held that beautiful and wanting young women wandered the aisles of Russo's in search of all the goods that frat-house guys like me offered in abundance. Sounds dumb now, but I believed it then. And because I believed it, I kept going back there and hanging around in sections where I thought the prettiest girls would be. Poetry, philosophy, self-improvement, art. Don't know why I believed girls were so attracted to poetry, philosophy, self-improvement, or art, but when I first saw Elizabeth she was reading from a thin little book of Spanish poems. So there.

That day, I knew. As the old song says, sometimes a man just knows. I knew this was My Elizabeth. My Elizabeth was tall and thin and blonde, warm and graceful as a spring breeze, and I knew. She had on sandals, loose jeans, and a pink blouse with the ugliest floral pattern I'd ever seen in my life, and she read poetry in a foreign language, and she loved things that I never cared about or knew existed, and still, I knew. My Elizabeth.

I ask again, "Can I have just one more?" but the bartender says, "Gotta close up, Gary. I'll get your tab," and then he looks at me like my nose just fell off. I don't say anything to him, though I do imagine picking up my glass and throwing it through his forehead. That would be fun. But instead, I shrug my shoulders, pick the glass up from the bar, and finish off my last gulp of gin and tonic.

Gary. He called me Gary. My name is not Gary. He knows my name is Vincent, has known that for God-knows how many years. Normally, I couldn't care less if he remembers my name or not, but now he wants to be all buddy-buddy with me and he can't remember my name and I hate that. He doesn't want to be my friend. I don't want him to be my friend. I'm just an unpaid tab to this guy, and he'll say whatever he thinks he needs to say to get that tab covered and me out the door without incident.

No doubt, he's afraid I'll try and skip out the door or take a swing at him when that check comes. Tonight, I drank twenty-six gin and tonics – I know because whenever I drink, I place each little black stirrer under my leg, to keep track, to keep from getting screwed – and maybe if another man drinks twenty-six gin and tonics he might be a load to handle. But I am not like another man. I am me, there's only one of me, I am polite and I am civilized and I've got this under control. I pay my tab, I pay a lot of tabs. Just bring me the bill so I can get out of here.

I reach for my wallet. It's thick with cash, more cash than this bartender makes in two months. And he thinks I won't pay my bill. Right.

The asshole brings the bill back to my end of the bar. "How much?" I say, taking the little white slip of paper from his hand before he can lay it down on the bar in front of me. I hate when they lay the tab face-down on the bar. It's like they're ashamed of the dollar amount. So rude – do they think I don't know exactly how much I drank? Guys like me, we always know the bill, not that it really matters, not that there's ever a danger we can't cover it.

"Thanks, Gary," he says. "I'll take it when you're ready. We close in ten minutes, okay?" Then he walks away again. I start to yell after him, start to inform him that I'm not Gary, I'm Vincent, I don't know Gary, shut up about Gary. But instead, I just check the tab, pull a hundred and twenty-five bucks out of my wallet, then throw in an extra fifty just to show the asshole that I can. Then I leave.

*

The day before our tenth wedding anniversary, Northeastern promoted me to *Vice President, Mortgage Division.* I'd worked a lot of long nights, made a lot of sacrifices – seventy hour weeks, no vacation in five years, things like that – and I deserved the recognition. The same night I got the news, I took Elizabeth to a restaurant downtown that we'd had our eye on for years, but never been able to afford, a strictly jacket-and-tie place on Broadway that was a little fancier than the one we'd planned for our anniversary dinner the next night, but which I thought was more than justified considering the special occasion.

This restaurant was the real deal. The kind of place where a tablecloth might cost more than an average man's suit, where a set of silverware was worth more than all the dishes we had in our house, and where reservations were most definitely required at least two weeks in advance. "But don't worry about that," I said to Elizabeth. "We'll get in." I promised that I would slip the guy in front a hundred dollar bill, get us in that way. We could afford to do things like that now. We could afford to pay what it took to get what we wanted. "Order whatever the hell you want, too. Anything," I said.

When we sat down at our table, I told the waiter to bring the most expensive bottle of cabernet sauvignon in the building. He looked at me funny (I guess people only order that way in movies) but he did as requested. To be honest, I never would have guessed that a single bottle of cabernet sauvignon, even one with such an unpronounceable name on the label, could cost that much. But it was worth it.

While we waited for our meal, I noticed that Elizabeth's gaze kept moving away from me and settling on whoever sat behind me. Finally, I asked, "What are you looking at?"

"What? I'm not looking at anything," she said.

"Are you sure?"

"I'm sure."

"Okay, then," I said. It was such a celebration; I didn't want a fight. I finished my glass of expensive cabernet, and then excused myself to the men's room. As I walked, though, I made a special effort to notice exactly who *was* seated behind me. I saw only a man in a dark brown suit, silver hair, maybe sixty years old. He sat by himself, reading the business pages, circling a few words here and there. The food on his plate was practically untouched.

When I got back to the table, I tried again. "You're sure you don't know that guy?" I asked Elizabeth.

"Which guy?" she said.

"The guy with the newspaper." I motioned towards him.

She looked behind me and shrugged. "Sorry, I don't know him. Why? You think he knows me?" She laughed. I picked up the wine, filled my glass again. I asked Elizabeth if she wanted any more, but she said she'd had enough. Which was fine – that just left more for me.

That night, we took a cab home because two glasses of wine was too much for Elizabeth, and also because I drank my share of that expensive cabernet sauvignon, then ordered another bottle and drank it all myself. The cab driver was a big fat guy who smelled like a rotten cigar and wore a Green Bay Packers t-shirt that was way too tight around the armpits. When we got to the driveway, Elizabeth asked the cabby if he could help carry me up the steps and into the house. On the way in, I rolled my head over onto his shoulder and puked expensive red wine all over that Packers shirt and also all over the side of the cabby's face, too. He didn't care much for that. Fortunately, though, we were already in the house at that point, and when he dropped me, I landed on the living room couch, which was soft black leather, brand new. Elizabeth gave the man fifty dollars on top of the fare for his troubles and said she was sorry I puked on him, that I got that way sometimes but that was pretty bad even for me. Then she helped me upstairs, undressed me and put me to bed and even kissed me on the forehead.

I remember that kiss. So soft, so warm, so perfect. The world spun and my brain sloshed inside my head like a rubber duck in a bathtub, but I remember that kiss.

"Goodnight, Vincent," I heard Elizabeth say, and then the world went dark.

Some time in the night, my dreams floated in on an ocean of red wine, dreams I didn't understand, dreams that maybe I didn't want to understand, and yet dreams that, somehow, I never forgot.. I saw so many things in my sleep that night. Business cards, stacked to the stars. A thousand empty houses, begging me to mortgage them to happy young couples. A solid oak desk, bought just for me, sitting in the middle of an office that was so big I had to take a taxi to get from one side to the other. I saw a fat cab driver in a Green Bay Packers shirt. I saw a bottle of cabernet sauvignon, tall as me, taller than me, the tallest and most expensive bottle of cabernet sauvignon in the whole world. I saw a silver-haired old man in a brown suit, sitting all alone in a restaurant, reading the business pages and circling things that interested him while his food rotted on the plate before him.

And I saw a girl.

A girl, a beautiful girl, tall and thin and blonde, warm and graceful as a spring breeze, wearing sandals, loose jeans, and a pink blouse with the prettiest floral pattern I could ever imagine. She stood in a bookstore. She asked if I liked poetry, and I said no, not really, and then she smiled and said that's fine, poetry isn't really all that important, anyway.

It's a nice night to stagger home drunk.

The warm wind keeps me from passing out on the sidewalk. I welcome the help. Since I walked out of the bar I've ascended three levels of drunkenness. Pine needles sneak up on you.

My house waits ahead. Our house. Her house. I wonder, is Elizabeth still awake? The lights are all turned off. I hope she's still awake. I feel the last seven hours rise out of my stomach, into my throat. Please be awake, Elizabeth. Please God, let her be awake.

I drop to my knees and throw up beside our mailbox.

Ten minutes later, I make it up the steps. I reach for the doorknob and find she's locked the door, but that doesn't make me mad. When you've got as much expensive stuff as we do, you keep the doors locked and the alarm system activated or else you'll wake up one morning and find you made a good Christmas for some sixteen year old shitass thief.

I knock on the door, quiet as I can. Don't want to be too loud, don't want to awaken the neighbors and damn sure don't want to set their damn dogs barking. The neighbors really hate that. I've awakened the neighbors and their damn dogs way too many times before, and the last time I did it they brought up the homeowner's association bylaws and threatened to toss us out of the neighborhood. I don't want to get tossed out of the neighborhood. It's such an expensive neighborhood.

I wait for a light to come on in the window, but no light comes on. I wait for Elizabeth to come and let me in. I wait. I wait. A long time I wait, half an hour, then a whole hour, but she doesn't come and she doesn't let me in. I stand on the porch until two-thirty in the morning, let the warm wind blow in my face, and enjoy the smell that rises from underneath my collar, the wonderful smell to which I have grown so accustomed: the sweet smell of pine needles.

Finally, sometime later but I'm not really sure *what* time, I hear footsteps inside the house. Coming down the stairs, into the living room. A light switches on, the door clicks open, and Elizabeth stands there in front of me. Her eyes are red, swollen, watery. She looks like she hasn't slept in a week. Maybe she hasn't. I think hard, hard as twenty-six gin and tonics will allow me. It's been a few hours since I left the bar but if there's one thing I've learned it's that those pine needles stick to you for a while.

I want to say the right thing. I'm not sure there is a right thing.

"Hello, Elizabeth," I say.

"I thought we agreed," says Elizabeth

She thinks we agreed? Agreed on what?

"You know exactly what, Vincent," Elizabeth says. I realize that I was thinking out loud again. Damn.

But the thing is, I *don't* know what. I never know what. And Elizabeth, she knows that I never know what. She thinks I don't know what because I just don't *want* to know what. Maybe there is some truth to that. I start to apologize, start to say I'm sorry, I don't know what, What? But Elizabeth holds up her hand and stops me. She wipes her puffy red eyes and stares at me for a long time. I don't know how long exactly, just that it's a long time, maybe the longest time we have ever gone like this, staring at each other, silent, unsure.

Then, her gaze jumps and settles on something or someone over my shoulder. I whip my head around, who's she looking at? Then I see him, for a shadowy moment. I see him. The man in the brown suit, the man with the silver hair, the man from our big expensive dinner all these years ago. The man in the brown suit with the newspaper spread out before him, the man who sits alone and quietly circles the interesting parts of the business section. I see him. I see him! What is he doing here now? Here with me, me and Elizabeth, my Elizabeth.

I reach for the man behind me. I want to know. I am drunk, too drunk. Still I turn from my beautiful Elizabeth, and reach for the man behind me, and open my mouth to ask what he's doing in the darkness, just beyond us. But by then, he's gone.

THE PRICE YOU PAY

by Kevin Hall

A stripper friend of mine recently tried to get me to pay her a visit at work. I mean this, of course, in the most literal of sense: she wanted me to drive to Lexington and hang out with her, all for the pre-determined costs selected by this particular establishment.

I politely declined, realizing it's a sad man who would pay money to talk to a hooker, a sadder man who would pay money to talk to a stripper.

Having never actually attended such a place, I found myself a bit intrigued by the setup, so before I officially rejected her offer, I asked a few questions. First, I should clarify: she's not really a stripper. She's a "waitress/dancer." I guess her clothes accidentally fall off. Perhaps she needs a better tailor.

In order to entice me to her business, she promised I would get in free and that she would waive the regular drink-minimum. Business was slow, she told me, meaning we could sit and talk for hours.

So long as I was willing to pay.

And how much, exactly, would it cost me to enjoy her dancing (or waitressing) and/or company?

"It's $15 a dance or three for $50," she said.

"Wouldn't I be better off buying three individual dances for $15 each, thus saving $5?" I asked.

"I don't set the prices, babe."

She then offered another option (one, I might add, that sounds highly more suspect): "You can have me for $200 for a half-hour or $500 an hour."

"Who sets your prices," I asked, "and have they ever even heard of math?"

I haven't heard from her since. I guess she's just busy with her calculator.

Live Nude Girls (or, How 6-Year Old Kevin Remained Totally Confused About Movies and Life)

by Kevin Hall

One of my favorite words is "nudity."

Take away the meaning of the word and any connotations that get attached to it, the word itself is amusing and can often generate laughs by itself, particularly when following the word "partial."

I've always been fond of the word, even long before I knew what it meant. In the earliest days of cable television in Powell County, subscribers would get little paper booklets from outlets like The Movie Channel (in those days, The Movie Channel was far more popular than HBO, thanks in large part to its tendency to show the Friday the 13th movies as often as possible) detailing the monthly schedule of movies.

(Partially Related Tangent, but Only Because It Involves the Early Days of Cable: In 1987, nothing in my life, and I truly mean nothing, was bigger than the WWF. Each year, Vince McMahon and company would get me excited for WrestleMania, which only had two viewing options: 1) pay per view; or 2) wait 8-12 months for the tape to arrive at Video Solution.

In the promos, the announcer would instruct us to call our cable companies today to order the pay per view, so that's exactly what I did. I'm 11 years old, calling Johnny Napier, Powell County's cable king, trying to order WrestleMania, then trying to figure out exactly why I couldn't get it in Stanton. Dejected, I would miss the wrestling event of the year (perhaps even of all time) and wake up the next morning, read the *Lexington Herald-Leader*'s sports section in hopes of finding the results, then calling the paper to find out who won the top matches, then trying to figure out exactly why it wasn't covered in the newspaper.)

Each day would have an hour-by-hour listing of movies, with the back of the guide providing, in alphabetical order, a brief description of each film. This handy feature also let you know the reason for a movie's rating, and to my young mind (I would have been about 6 years old), I always stayed puzzled by the explanations.

Language: What movie wouldn't have some sort of language in it? How else would these people communicate? I found it puzzling that a movie could get rated R simply for the use of language.

Violence: OK, so this one made sense. I'm an American; I understand violence in pop culture.

Adult Situations: To a 6-year-old, pretty much everything is an adult situation, which when read literally, as my mind did, is a situation between adults. A professional baseball game involved nine innings of adult situations. For heaven's sake, church was chock full of adult situations (the exception, of course, being Youth Sunday). I was 6; I didn't understand the concept of "sex" and certainly failed to grasp the importance of "adult situations." I wonder how many movies I skipped because I saw they featured "adult situations" and thought "Great ... another movie with adults talking about filing their taxes."

Nudity: I knew what nudity was, making me feel like the most sophisticated kid in Sophisticateville. Unfortunately, I knew neither the actual meaning nor the proper pronunciation.

I thought *new-duh-tee* was pronounced *nuh-duh-tee*, and before I continue, I again remind you I was about 6 years old. "Nudity" was not one of Mrs. Lake's regular words in our kindergarten class.

So, what exactly did "nudity/nuh-duh-tee" mean? I had it figured out:

It's when a movie featured really silly things, like people acting, and I'm serious about this, nutty. Hence, nuttity. Hence, nuh-duh-tee. Hence, nudity.

I'm fairly certain I explained my rationale to my family at some point, and while I'm sure they appreciated knowing their little boy wasn't going to be watching some nudity-filled sex romp, I'm quite positive they appreciated even more knowing their little boy was a naïve turd.

A DARK ROOM

A short play by Kevin Hall

A dark room, nothing visible. A noise, muffled, sounds vaguely human. Outside, a train whistle blows, long, loud. Dogs bark, their cries chasing after the whistle before both sounds fade off, leaving everything again as quiet as it is dark.

A small light, numbers on a clock. Mumbling under someone's breath. Items knock around on a table as a hand become visible in the faint glow. It picks up a small cell phone, turns it on. More light, with a few shapes now visible: a small table, a book, a clock, a bed. The cell phone light shuts off, back to total darkness.

A voice, male, early 30s, tired, speaks.

Voice: Every night. Every fucking night.

Shuffling in the bed, covers rustling, moving, twisting.

Voice: God, what can I do? No, really, God, I'm asking, what can I do? I'm literally on my hands and knees here, wondering. (pause) OK, I'm not *really* on my hands and knees, but let's focus on what's real here. Let's focus, God, on the issue at hand, the reason I'm here, 3:47 a.m., talking to myself, hoping that somewhere on the other side, somewhere over there there's a mystic connection and you just happen to be listening.

More shuffling. Feet land on hardwood.

Voice: Is it me, God? It is, isn't it? So what is it about me, what is it about me that just doesn't measure up, just somehow always falls short, never quite reaches it out? Can you tell me that? Can I be cliché, say "give me a sign"? Well, you've given me signs. I've seen them. I've just usually chosen to ignore them. I know you're God and everything, and there's this level of almighty-ness that comes with it, but sometimes I guess my freewill pulls some rank. I mean, the choice is mine, right?

Joints pop and crack as he stands.
Voice: Maybe that's what I'm doing wrong. Following my own advice.

He begins walking in the dark.

Voice: I have to get stronger, though. Right? I mean, I will, right? You can't let me keep on like this, up at all hours, stressing over everything that happened. Right? You'll help me let go. Right? I just want to move on. I just want to feel whole. I just want my brain to rest for a bit, even if it just a day, instead of whirring around nonstop, replaying all that's happened, rethinking everything that's been said.

A whirring noise, followed by a bright light illuminating the room. A computer comes to life. He sits down, begins to type as he checks his e-mail.

Voice: I'm sorry I pushed her away. There was this gift, this amazing person, right there, ready for me, and I couldn't handle it. You put her there, knowing what I needed, but, I guess, knowing eventually I wouldn't let it work. Was that a joke, some sort of cosmic comedy you got going on up there? It's not funny, that's for sure. (pause) No, I know. I know. It's not you. Really. It's me. It's my problem. (pause) But I need your help.

The computer turns off. He remains seated in the dark.

Voice: I don't know what to do. It's all I think about. *She's* all I think about. What went wrong. Even what went right. It keeps me busy. But I don't want to be busy anymore. I just want to rest.

He stands, walks off, trailed by the sound of his rustling pajamas. Bare feet sound against the hardwood floor.

Voice: I want your strength. Not *your* strength, the strength of God, but strength *from* God, the strength to keep on, the strength to make it through each day. Right now, actually, I'll settle for the strength to make it out of bed in the morning. From there, we'll negotiate.

He stops. A door opens. A refrigerator. The glow fills the room. He reaches in, grabs a carton of milk. Shuts the door, but not all the way, allowing the light to shine a bit.

Voice: But strength, in one form or another, short-term for now, long-term for later, that would be good. I'd like that. I need that. (pause) Please.

A cupboard opens, a cup comes out.

Voice: And let me be OK. Let me get through this, day after day.

The milk pours into the cup, stops. He takes a drink, sighs. Takes another drink.

Voice: And, I guess, be with her, too.

He puts the milk back in the refrigerator, shuts the door. Darkness.

Voice: Wherever she is.

He walks off. Bare feet sound against the hardwood floor.

Voice: I've tried so long to do what you want, to do the right thing. I know I still am, but I just hope it pays off, and sooner rather than later. I'm tired. I'm tired of feeling alone. I'm tired of being alone. (pause) And I'm tired of feeling like I'm always complaining about being alone.

The bed squeaks as he sits down, returns to attempt to sleep. Covers rustle as he nestles in.

Voice: But I know you're there, and I know you have a plan. I just wish you'd clue me in, give some sort of sign (pause) and not one that I'll ignore.

He yawns.

Voice: I guess I'm pretty selfish. All this fighting, the storms, the death, the war, and here I am talking about my petty life, my heartache.

He yawns. His voice slows, growing tired.

Voice: But I know you care. My problems are real to me. I'm not crazy. I'm not exhausting. I'm a good person …

… a good person …

… a good person …

… a good …

… person.

He's asleep. A dark room. Quiet.

Seconds pass. Five. Ten. Twenty. A minute. Two. A train whistle blows, long, loud. Dogs bark.

Voice: Every night. Every fucking night.

WERE YOU RAISED IN A BARNES (AND NOBLE)? B&N GETS AN "F" FOR CUSTOMER SERVICE

by Kevin Hall

Note: This is built out of a month of frustration, anger and general disappointment, so some adult language will likely follow.

Barnes & Noble can go straight to the fieriest depths of hell, which is, of course, a complete impossibility, but not because it's a corporate entity already devoid of a soul but because the company is, I'm quite positive, hell itself.

I've not always felt this way. As recently as five weeks ago, I championed the company, even to the point of recommending Barnes & Noble's e-reader, the nook, over the market leader, the Amazon Kindle.

Oh, but then came four weeks ago, at which point the cracks in my long-standing appreciation of Barnes & Noble began to show, culminating in a full-out divorce following things I discovered on Tuesday. I share them with you now, in part to vent, but mostly to caution others who might be considering venturing into the nook world. I hope you will think long and hard against it, opting instead for wiser investments, such as the Kindle or simply tossing your cash out a window and watching it scatter off in the wind.

I spend the bulk of my daily lunch break reading, getting at least a good 45 minutes in before it's time to start back to the grind. This one particular Thursday, as I got out my nook and prepared to get lost into a new story, I discovered the device had, without warning, completely reset itself, thus causing me to have to re-register the device.

This wouldn't have been a problem, but my work doesn't have a public wi-fi connection, so I had to wait until I returned home. This wouldn't have been a problem, but my home wi-fi simply wouldn't connect, no matter how many times I tried. I did some trouble-shooting with other devices, and everyone connected without a problem, and my password worked, leaving the fault lying with the nook.

I called customer service, explained the problem, got transferred to the nook technical support, explained the problem again and finally got a bit of help from a friendly representative. The only problem with him, though, was when he said his solution would work "10 out of 10 times," leading me to believe that I had pretty good odds of it actually working.

It did not.

I called back, only this time, I began my descent through what has become the single worst (and longest) customer experience service in my life. The first person who answered could not be understood. This had less to do with the fact he spoke unintelligible English (although that certainly didn't help) and more to do with the fact it sounded as though he was sitting in The Loudest Spot on the Planet.

Have you ever called someone who was in a crowded bar or at a concert, and no matter how loudly that person talks, you simply can't hear much of what they're saying over the din in the background? This was like that, only somehow louder and more annoying.

I asked the rep repeatedly if perhaps something could be done about the noise, but my pleas fell on deaf ears. I mean that quite literally; I doubt he was able to hear me.

He tried to help me, mostly by instructing me to turn the device off and then back on again. He repeated this four more times, none of which proved even slightly more effective than the previous times, unless you include its effectiveness in making me angry.

As he tried again (a sixth time total!) to have me shut the nook off and then on, I snapped.

"How many times can you ask me to do this and think it's going to do ANYTHING different at all?" I asked, my voice raising.

"Sir, it is what the manual suggests."

"Six times? SIX TIMES?!? Does it REALLY say that the customer should turn it off and on to infinity, or does it perhaps say that it might work after 17 times? Is that our goal?"

"Sir, I'm simply trying to help."

"You are failing greatly at that. Also, I can't take this noise any longer. I need to speak to someone else."

He placed me on hold, where I waited for over 10 minutes. Barnes & Noble also has terrible hold music. They really need to improve that.

Finally, another rep got on the line, and after a quick review of the problem, he offered a sure-fire solution: "OK, sir, can you please shut the device off and turn it back on?"

I'm not sure what a wolfman feels like the morning after having turned into a wolfman, having terrorized a town at night only to wake up the next morning, back in human form, fairly certain things got out of hand but without a totally clear recollection.

I say that because I went full wolfman on the rep. I don't recall everything, but there was some yelling, some vague threats, some very specific suggestions and some salty language.

I finally just asked if it wouldn't be easier for me to take the damaged nook to a brick-and-mortar Barnes & Noble store and have it replaced.

The rep agreed, telling me I'd get an email shortly thereafter allowing me to trade in my nook for a refurbished model. I wasn't too happy about getting a used product, but that's how their warranty works after 30 days, and, well, a used nook was better than the one I had which didn't work at all.

By the next evening, I had the replacement nook in hand, back at my house and ready to get everything set up and working. The nook, however, had other ideas, choosing instead to have the exact same problem connecting to wi-fi that my previous one had. Instead of suffering through another call with B&N's customer service, I searched online and learned several others had experienced a similar problem after switching to AT&T U-Verse for their internet service. This seemed odd because I had asked the technical support person exactly that and was told he'd never heard of such a problem.

I followed the advice on a forum (found on the B&N website, mind you, which maybe the tech support guy should perhaps be familiar with), and fixed the problem in under two minutes.

In order to help others who might be having a problem with this (OK, it was to actually be a smart ass, but whatever), I called the B&N support team and told them about both the problem and the very simple solution.

"Oh, that's actually the first thing we ask people who have the connectivity problem," this rep told me.

I'm pretty sure I howled.

I am a fan of the author Frank Bill. He writes gritty stories about towns similar to the one I grew up in, and the fact he's from southern Indiana (near Louisville, I do believe) only makes it that much better. Last week, I couldn't wait to download his new novel, *Donnybrook*, and get to reading it over the weekend.

I downloaded it Wednesday night but didn't open it because I was finishing up another novel. By the time my Thursday lunch break rolled around, I was anxious to open it, so imagine my surprise when despite clicking on a picture of the *Donnybrook* cover, the book that actually opened was a romance novel called *Wed to a Highland Warrior*.

I begrudgingly called B&N's customer service line, and again was met with some lackluster customer service. This time, the rep (who appeared to be in a non-U.S. call center) had trouble accepting my claim from the start.

After I'd explained the situation, he said this: "So to recap, you downloaded the wrong book and need help getting the correct one?"

Um, no.

I tried explaining again, and he read his answers back to me from his manual and assured me that everything should be OK, despite heavily implying he didn't believe me. He later confirmed this by saying he tried downloading the book on his own, only to see that it opened without a problem.

While this was going on, I took to Twitter to contact the author, who almost immediately wrote back and said I was the second person to have reported that exact problem to him. Look, no offense to Mr. Bill (again, I think he's an excellent writer), but it's not as if his book is a massive bestseller. If two people had reported the same problem downloading the book on their nook, it's highly likely that those were the ONLY two people who had downloaded them on their nook.

Yet Barnes & Noble assured me it wasn't a problem.

The rep, however, told me he'd refund my money and I could try downloading it again in two weeks. He never gave me a clear indication as to why I'd need to wait two weeks, but I also knew I wouldn't wait that long because I wanted to read the book now, and this is America and we have no patience.

I ended up ordering a hardcopy of the book (it arrived Monday, and let me tell you, so far, *Donnybrook* is amazing), and by all accounts my money was refunded. It would have stopped there had it not been for another Twitter message from the author telling me he'd contacted his publisher and the problem was being resolved.

I called B&N back to find out why I'd been given such poor information, and this time the rep tried telling me he could fix everything simply by archiving and then re-opening the original purchase. One problem: the first rep had already deleted my book after giving the refund (which is a perfectly reasonable thing to do). This rep, though, couldn't understand why the first guy even suggested that because a) it could've been fixed in a much easier fashion; and b) for reasons I still don't understand, once you download a book, if it gets returned you can never download it again.

A hundred monkeys (particularly those dressed in vests) would likely provide better service, and that factors in their proclivity to toss their own poop.

I decided to try one more thing: I asked the guy if any downloaded version of *Donnybrook* from Barnes & Noble would work, or if they'd all default to *Wed to a Highland Warrior*. The rep explained that because the mistake was from the publishing company, all would open incorrectly. I asked him to humor me and try downloading it, which he did, and, of course, it opened as *Wed to a Highland Warrior*, meaning the original rep who claimed to have downloaded it was, in fact, lying.

I wrote an email to Barnes & Noble's customer service center, fully explaining my problems and asking for someone to at least attempt to provide some sort of rationale behind all the bad advice I'd been given. Their answer skirted all issues raised, choosing instead to say they're shocked because they usually have great customer service. This led to a response of my own:

I really find Barnes & Noble's response to be lacking. Other than my money being refunded, which frankly isn't something you should be applauded because you kinda have to give the money back, you've done zilch to try to make this better. I'm not a customer service expert (also, neither is anyone I've spoken with at Barnes & Noble), but here's what I would have done after a certain level of customer dissatisfaction: "Sir, we apologize for all the problems, and in an effort to try to make it right, we have provided you with a copy of the book in question, at our cost, in your Nook library. Please enjoy."

However, that would be a waste of time at this point because I already have the book through other means.

I also want to point out the absurdity of this statement: "The level of service you received is unusual, as we are accustomed to providing the highest quality customer service at all times." I'm fairly certain you are confused as to the meaning of the words "unusual" and "highest quality," because the last two major issues I've had with Barnes & Noble have been met with the lowest quality of customer service, which to me makes this quite usual.

To help, try this: http://www.amazon.com/Merriam-Websters-Collegiate-Dictionary-Edition-ebook/dp/B000SEGJ5S/ref=sr_1_4?s=digital-text&ie=UTF8&qid=1362757226&sr=1-4&keywords=dictionary. When you download it, I hope you actually get the book you ordered. It's frustrating when you don't.

In summation, fuck that noise.

Yours very truly,
Kevin Hall

They sent me a $15 gift card.

This past Monday, I received an email from Barnes & Noble saying that in order to process the return of my nook, I would need to contact them with a return authorization code provided in the email.

Seeing as how I had not attempted to return this nook, I found this email puzzling. I replied to it with a simple "Um, what?" and sent a longer email to Dan, a customer service rep with whom I'd previously spoken. Neither of my messages have yet to receive a reply.

On Tuesday, I spent the better part of my lunch break on the phone with various B&N customer service reps, trying to determine why I'd received this mysterious email, and no one could offer much help. Finally, after about 35 minutes on the phone, one rep said my account showed that I'd attempted to purchase a new nook at 5:40 p.m. on Monday.

I assured her I had not.

It was at this point I lost all interest in civility with Barnes & Noble, because someone somewhere had started messing with my account. This is definitely not acceptable, as I told the rep, who said she understood what I was feeling. I told her that I had just learned an unauthorized purchase had been attempted on my account, so I really doubted she fully understood what I was feeling unless she understood that I wanted to reach through the phone and start beating people with all the non-working nooks the company no doubt has in storage.

She gave me a number for the sales auditing department, saying they'd be able to assist me.

Tuesday afternoon, I called that department, and after going through everything again, the rep told me they couldn't help me and that I'd need to call customer service.

"They told me to call you!" I told her.

"I'm not sure why they did that because they would be the ones to help you. Nothing in our records shows anything on your account. I'll transfer you back to them."

I think the full moon returned.

"Now you listen to me, and you listen good. You will do nothing of the such. You are going to call them yourself and find out why their computer shows an attempted purchase at 5:40 p.m. and your computer shows nothing. Then you're going to explain to me just what, exactly, Barnes & Noble is going to do to make this right."

She at least tried.

The explanation was something along the lines of this: when I returned my nook, the company didn't completely deregister the device. In the time since I returned it, someone else has bought it and has now returned it, and when they did, I got an email processing the return.

"So, to be clear, your company failed to completely wipe off all my information from my old nook?"

"That seems to be the case, yes."

"You see how that's a problem?"

"Yes, and to make it right, you have my word we will clear that information now as we switch the registration."

"You understand that your word means nothing to me, right? I mean, your company is fully of liars and morons and I'm still wondering how you're going to make this right."

"You need to talk to our customer service for that."

"No, I need the number for your legal department for that."

"We aren't authorized to transfer calls to them."

Fortunately, there's this invention called "Google," and it's not difficult at all to find B&N's legal contact. I prepared a brief email for them, and I think it is about the only way this saga can end:

Dear Barnes and Noble lawyers: I plan on shipping you a fine collection of turds. Most will be of a human origin, but rest assured there will be a mix of cat and dog feces in there as well. I need to know, however, if you prefer UPS or FedEx.

Respectfully,
Kevin Hall
P.S. I will be eating lots of corn.

MEET ME AT THE MONKEY BARS

by Kevin Hall

Dear Laura,

I'm sorry I didn't kiss you back. The timing was severely awkward, and to be quite honest, I've never been much of a fan of public displays of affection. With everyone standing around watching, I would have been far too self-conscious, and I'm not sure you would have been pleased with the end result.

Plus, I was only 5 years old.

That's really gotta count for something, in my defense. Sure, you were the same age, but I was small for my age, and you towered over me. And, anyhow, girls mature faster than boys.

I hope that now you don't hold it against me. I guess we're, what, 27 years later, so it's doubtful you still hold a grudge. Just know that it wasn't because you weren't pretty, because you were. You had the prettiest long hair in school, and I mean that. Other girls, well, they just had long hair that trailed off down below their asses, just hanging there limp like a novelty, but you, you Laura, you did something with it. It sparkled, although I'm sure our arts and crafts time probably helped fill it with glitter, but to me, it was pure stardust. I'm not sure what you did to it — maybe just brushed it — but it worked.

I also liked that you smelled like glue.

Anyway, Laura, I hope you're doing well and have found someone who will kiss you underneath the monkey bars. Me? Well, I'm still looking. Maybe I'll try the swing set …

Sincerely,

P.S. I should probably clarify that I didn't mean a literal swing set. I don't regularly pick up women (or kids, for that matter) at the neighborhood playgrounds. So please don't think awful of me.

P.S.S. Reading back, I see again where I should note that I was kidding about picking up kids at a playground. I shouldn't joke about that. As far as I know, you could've had a child molested or kidnapped from a playground, and my attempts at humor are only bringing back those terrible memories. Which, I guess, I'm also doing here by keeping on talking about it. Except allow me to say, if you did have a kid stolen (I know that you don't "steal" a child, but it would have been odd to have had "kid" and "kidnapped" right next to each other, although I guess I could have gone with "child" and "kidnapped" instead), I hope you and your family have healed from the loss and have had more kids to replace him. Or her, I guess, if it was a girl.

And if you didn't suffer a kidnapping, congratulations!

Best wishes.

ONE WRECK TO RULE THEM ALL

by Kevin Hall

My grandmother's brains splattered across the dashboard.

Slumped over in her seat with her right cheek pressed against the vinyl, she looked at rest, almost peaceful even, as she lay there dying or, perhaps more likely, dead. A thought struck my mind — *Those are Granny's brains* — instantly and clearly, lodging there just long enough for recognition of the situation before scampering off wherever it is stray thoughts go.

I smelled something not quite recognizable, at least not at first, but really, it's not like I should have known at 11 years old what my great-aunt's flesh and hair would smell like as it burned. Sitting in the back seat, directly behind Granny, my great-aunt (and my granny's sister) had been thrown forward upon impact, her right forearm pushing across the door's armrest. The carpet and her flesh did not mesh well, as the friction seemed to melt the skin and singe the hair, creating a smell that threatened to overtake the rest of the car.

It happened fast, but that's what every car wreck survivor says. "In the blink of an eye ..." "Before I knew it ..." "Never saw it coming ..." They all say it, of course, but I wonder how much of it is true. For me, it did happen fast, in real time, but just like another post-wreck cliché, it unfolded in slow motion.

We — Mom, Granny, my great-aunt, my cousin and me — were coming home from Ohio, returning with my cousin (and her cat) so she could visit my grandparents for a few days. All had gone well for the first 200-plus miles of the trip, but Mount Sterling's bypass had other plans. An elderly couple, whose vision was partially blocked by a small hill to their left, pulled out in front of Mom's Oldsmobile Cutlass. From my spot in the backseat, in the middle between my cousin (and her cat) and my great-aunt, I watched it all unfold, the windshield serving like a widescreen TV that probably hadn't even been invented yet.

To my left (the view partially obscured by the top of Mom's head, her curly hair mixing in with the scenery), I could see businesses, probably strip malls, the kind that pop up along almost every highway in mid-sized Kentucky towns, full of video stores, Chinese food, maybe even a pharmacy. Straight ahead found us met by road, two lanes on each side, a wide median in the middle, and enough of a straight stretch to generate a little extra speed. At right, a few houses, stray roads, slight hills.

The car came from our right. I'm pretty sure they never saw us, not even at impact. I count that as a little victory for them. Here's what they missed:

•Time slowing down, slower than imaginable, stretching from seconds into apparent minutes before impact.

•A moment, however brief, of praying they speed up enough to make it through the intersection in time.

• The realization they would not.

• Brakes, loud and harsh, squalling against the asphalt, the tires pleading with the car, "Stop, stop, oh God, please stop."

• The crunch of wreck, metal and fiberglass and rubber and everything else, colliding as we rammed straight on into the driver's side door.

• The windshield spider-webbing, from forces both outside and inside the car.

• Temporary blackness.

Then came the chaos.

Beyond the brains and the burning, I had to immediately deal with a very pissed off cat, who somehow ended up thrown onto me, where it instinctively released all its claws deep into my forearm, latching itself in a death grip that later required a tetanus shot, just to be safe. The cat hung from my arm as I tried to shake it off, but it wouldn't let go, at least not at first. After about 10 seconds of bonding with my arm, it released and ran off in a white streak across the road. We never saw that cat again. It left scars on me for more than 10 years, though.

Mom stood in the road, punch-drunk on her feet, trying (and failing) to get cars to stop to help. She begged, a voice so raw and ragged I hoped then never to hear anything like it again. The cars drove past, oblivious to Mom's cries detailing Granny's previously broken hips and other health woes.

I had been thrown forward from my perch in the middle (one, I might add, that was not equipped with a seatbelt, not that it would have been in use at that point in 1987). My shins saved me from being launched into the front, most likely into (and through) the windshield. Each leg slammed into the front seat on each side, keeping me secure in the backseat. When I woke up the morning after, both legs, literally from knee to ankle, were the deep purple of a late-evening thunderstorm, but in the immediate aftermath of the wreck, I felt nothing. Adrenaline, it seems, is a blessing.

I ran across the two lanes of traffic, looking for someone, anyone, who could help. About two houses down, a man in headphones worked on his lawn, mowing in the sunlight, completely unaware at what had happened a few hundred feet away. I don't recall what I told him, but it must have been rather effective: he ushered me inside and called 911 and got ambulances on the way to the scene. He helped me call my dad, and I tried to explain what had happened and where we were. I hung up the phone and sprinted back to the accident scene.

Mom tried to tell the ambulance drivers and police the details, but it's likely she had gone into complete shock at this point. I helped with some basic information – what happened, birthdays, addresses, ages, things of that sort — but most of that came later as more family arrived at the hospital.

I don't recall how I got to the hospital – it might have been in an ambulance, it might have been in a friend's truck. I remained too distracted then and through the rest of the night, even much later at my other grandparents' house (I remember watching the made-for-TV movie *Escape from Sobibor* and really enjoying it; I also might have been in shock) to have a fully functioning brain. Instead, I found myself analyzing and obsessing over every detail that happened before that led to the wreck.

In Ohio, I had pushed for a stop for ice cream. Had we not stopped that extra 10 minutes, we would have passed through Mount Sterling earlier, thus avoiding the wreck, I told myself.

I used the restroom at the restaurant, a Rax's (I don't see many these days, but when I do, the wreck flashbacks hit hard; I also see "Rax's" and "wrecks" and wonder how much of the day might have been destined by fate). If only I had washed my hands longer after peeing (or, more truthfully, being an 11-year-old boy, had I just not washed them at all), maybe we would have had 20 extra seconds in which to avoid the wreck.

Eleven years old with the weight of the family on my shoulders. I blamed myself for years.

I guess I should have eased up on myself. My mom ended up unhurt (and I still don't know how she ended up, at least physically, injury-free), my cousin escaped without a single bruise and my great-aunt had a full recovery.

As for my grandmother, she also eventually healed — it turns out those weren't brains at all. She, too, had enjoyed a milkshake in Ohio, and the leftover ice cream had been thrown from the cup and onto the dash, giving an unfortunate illusion. In hindsight, I guess I should have realized that was my grandmother's brains.

APEP, THE DARKNESS

by Aaron Saylor

Underneath the antique shop, in the heart of ancient Cairo, Agent Kurtzberg follows Hassan down the darkened corridor. Flickering torches light the way, mounted in the stone walls every fifteen feet or so, throwing just enough light to catch the twitchy figures of rats as they scurry along the floor. Mold chokes the atmosphere; from the craggy look of the rock walls and the depth of the filth on their surface, Kurtzberg figures this corridor must have been tunneled out a hundred years ago, at least.

Considering the part of the world in which he finds himself, the American agent halfway expects a mummy to shuffle by at any moment, dragging its cursed bandages behind.

Maybe twenty yards down, a faint orange glow from the right side signals a bend in the corridor and an opening to a large room. Muffled sounds emanate from there, suggesting a human presence: the occasional clank of metal on metal, hushed voices.

Then – a scream.

A *scream!*

The shrill cry of agony rips through the corridor like a scimitar through the belly of an antelope. Hassan moves forward, unfazed, but the wail stops Kurtzberg cold. It rattles the air for five or six seconds – seconds that feel like decades to the unnerved agent.

"What... was *that?*" he whispers.

Hassan turns, makes blank eye contact, but doesn't say a word. He doesn't shrug, he doesn't look surprised, he doesn't look like he cares, he doesn't look like anything. Then he straightens back around and keeps walking.

Soon, though, the scream fades. A few moments after it's gone, another man appears, walking away from the room around the bend. He's wearing a dirty white robe and sandals. His head is shaved smooth. He comes towards them, slow, unconcerned that they are there. He carries a small swaddle in his arms that hides something Kurtzberg can't quite identify at such distance.

As this bald man approaches, the agent's nerves dance. Kurtzberg thinks about the pistol strapped against his chest. But the closer the man gets, the more Carl realizes that the gun won't be necessary right now. This man has no intention of confronting them. This man doesn't even know they are there. He stares straight ahead, past them, into the beyond. Finally he is just a few feet away, and when he brushes numbly past, the agent realizes what is inside the swaddle that the approaching man holds in his arms. A small child.

Earlier that night. Not long ago at all.

Carl Kurtzberg stares through the grimy windshield of his automobile. *It's all so familiar*, he thinks, as he looks into the shimmering Egyptian night. *Been here, done this, gonna do it again someday.*

Six months ago, the telephone communication went abruptly silent between antiques dealer Hassan al-Ramin and his Syrian friend Salah Aziz, following a month of heightened and easily-decoded chatter regarding natural gas pipelines across Texas and Louisiana. This made the Agency nervous, so they instructed Kurtzberg to find Hassan. After all, finding people is Kurtzberg's special talent – a talent honed to perfection by a decade's work across northern Africa and the Middle East, stalking through darkened streets and alleys not at all unlike the street and alley before him now. It's all so familiar, the way he feels now – the heat, the hazy lights, the air thick with dust, the warm sweat gilding the back of his neck as he sits in his car waiting for someone he has seen only in satellite photographs. It's all so familiar.

Here, tonight, Kurtzberg waits, just a few yards from the rather shabby facade of Hassan al-Ramin's antique shop. People walk around the Agency man's car, unnoticing, unconcerned. He peers into the night, looking for one shadow in the aimless tangle of shadows that descends backward into the alley, ever folding into the hopelessness of urban decay.

The agent breathes deep. His twelve-year-old BMW carries the musty and permanent odor of hand-rolled cigarettes, absorbed into the cracked dashboard and the pores of the tan leather seats. It's a comfortable smell, reminiscent of Tennessee, of October afternoons with friends in the schoolyard, sneaking smokes behind old oak trees. Kurtzberg doesn't own the vehicle – it actually belongs to Rhameini, the jeweler deemed by the Agency as primary liaison for this sector of the city – but all Carl Kurtzberg knows is that it smells like tobacco and Tennessee and reminds him of home and that is what matters.

Three hours ago, as the sun sank in the sky, he pulled into this spot alongside the curb, where he can see the shop entrance and everyone who walks through it. Now he tap tap taps on the dashboard to keep himself awake. He checks his shiny silver Tag Heuer wristwatch and finds midnight just thirty-two minutes away. With one hand, Kurtzberg holds his black iphone to his ear. He doesn't speak into it, though, nor does anybody speak to him, either. This is another part of the ruse: he gives the impression of conversation only for the benefit of those who see him. He must maintain the ruse. He is not here for conversation. He is here for Hassan. He must maintain the ruse.

Even with the BMW and the Tag Heuer and the iphone, the agent seems to passers-by that he is just another shadow among them, indistinguishable from all the other shadows in Cairo. His dusky skin glistens with night sweat. Black stubble covers his face; thick black curls of hair poke out around the edges of the Yankees baseball cap pulled down tight on his head. He wears a grey, unremarkable t-shirt and unremarkable blue jeans. He looks like an unremarkable man. He looks like he belongs in this steamy place, which of course is why the Agency sent him here.

Lazy light emanates from the streetlamps lining the block. Every third or fourth one is broken. People wander the street, shambling all around Kurtzberg as if they are the walking dead loosed from a midnight horror film. Men, women, children. Merchants, tourists, citizens, beggars, thieves. Shadows. Ghosts. Hassan.

Hassan! There!

Kurtzberg spies his target: a small man, no more than five and a half feet tall, roaming amidst the aimless shades, toward the tinted glass doors of Hassan's Antique Shop, the business that bears his name in golden Arabic letters six inches high. They have met twenty-seven times in the past six months, as Carl worked to forge confidence with the Egyptian and gain a face-to-face with Salah Aziz. The agent is completely familiar with Hassan's look. *It's all so familiar.*

As Hassan ducks into his shop, the agent notices two young girls who cannot be far removed from their teen years. The youths stand to one side of the broken concrete steps that rise to the shop entrance. These girls are close enough to Kurtzberg that he can make out their sallow skin and dark, hollow eyes. With shaky hands they exchange gifts: one girl hands the other a fistful of sheqels – what looks to Kurtzberg like the rough equivalent of two hundred American dollars – and in return, she receives a small falcon statuette that is nearly the length of her forearm. After a quick look around, she removes the bird's ceramic head and takes out the real prize: two pill bottles. And while Kurtzberg doesn't actually see the contents of the bottles, he knows what is in them. The red pills are in them.

Kurtzberg knows the red pills well.

But he is here for al-Ramin.

The unremarkable agent in his t-shirt and jeans climbs out of his car and makes his way across the street towards Hassan's Antique Shop, through the slippery silhouettes that fill the alleyway even at this night hour. The citizens, the tourists, the beggars, the ghosts. The girls with the sheqels and the falcon statuette, the girls with their red pills, the girls, the girls, the girls.

He ascends the steps and opens the glass door. The girls pay him no mind as he moves past.

Inside, Carl Kurtzberg finds that the atmosphere of this place weighs down on him, full of history and dread. The place is part museum, part ancient pharmacy. Relics jut towards him at odd angles, crammed into every inch of available space that the room has to offer. Hand-woven rugs. Oil lamps made of dirty crystal. Books with slippery bindings. Paintings of olive groves, children playing, and moonlit city streets. A suit of vaguely European armor. More, and more, and more, a vast sea of antiquities. So many old things, occupying the heavy space around the agent.

The agent glances around the rectangular room, looking for Hassan but not finding him or any trace of him. The room is not large, maybe seven meters wide and fifteen meters long. There are only four corners and few places to hide between them. The antique dealer walked inside less than two minutes ago; he could not have simply vanished. And yet he seems to have done just that.

Kurtzberg has no worries, though. Finding people is his special talent. He will find Hassan. He moves through the shop, careful not to make any noise or disturb any of the artifacts, careful not to be seen by anyone that he doesn't wish to see him. If the wrong person sees the agent the entire operation will crumble. With al-Ramin so close it would be difficult to swallow failure now.

Two rows of bookshelves create a corridor down the entire left side of the room and he heads there, thinking he can disappear among the volumes and perhaps find a better vantage point from which to look for other exits.

He walks down the row, absently scanning the shelves, pretending to be interested in the wonders they contain. Some have handsome covers, their titles hand-painted with golden lettering or stamped in metallic foil, some bound with leather, others with sheepskin, still others with fraying cloth dyed one of many colors, violets, reds, greens, browns, indigos. He passes books about weaponry, cooking, human anatomy, agriculture, and botany. Books of maps which, if opened, would show places with names that have not been spoken in three centuries, on continents long consigned to myth. Atlantis, Hyperborea, Kumari Kundam. In truth, if Carl Kurtzberg opened any of those books he would wonder what they were doing here, on a dusty shelf in the antique shop of Hassan al-Ramin, rather than behind guarded glass in some far-off museum. But he moves on.

The agent strolls quietly towards the back of the shop, looking for a veil doorway or other exit that might have earlier escaped his glances. He does his best to maintain disinterest in the more exotic surroundings. He must be ready if Hassan should appear.

But despite Kurtzberg's best efforts, a tome catches his attention: one much bigger than the rest, with thick pages bound in cracking red leather. The book rests about halfway down the row, alone on a shelf near his waist. It is unencumbered by other books, as though it deserved a special place even in a room full of priceless, special things.

The book lays propped open to its exact center. The pages look strangely supple, the colors bright and clear, more bright and clear than a book of its age has any right to be. It shows a two-page reproduction of a painting unmistakably Egyptian in origin. Kurtzberg stops and turns toward the image. He sees an army, bronze-skinned men with long spears, engaged in battle with monsters possessing the bodies of men but the heads of hooded cobras. The cobra men devour soldiers whole. Crimson blood sprays in great plumes, across the ground from the monsters' mouths and from their victims' torn bodies. Men and monsters thrash each other, awash in the red stuff.

Black hieroglyphics scrawl across the bottom of the picture, pictographs showing birds and snakes and wavy lines like water and other images that Kurtzberg can't quite make out. It wouldn't matter if he *could* make them out.

"Apep," says a voice behind him.

The agent turns around and finds Hassan standing just over his shoulder, not two steps back.

"I'm sorry," Kurtzberg says. "I didn't see you –"

Hassan steps around him, pointing at the picture of soldiers and snake monsters. "This is the book of Apep. The snake. The darkness." He traces his finger along the hieroglyphics, translating as he goes. "'The snake encircles the world. Across all eternity, he rises each night, commanding his demons in battle against the noble Sun God, for only the Sun God shall defeat him.'"

He pauses, looks at Carl, then smiles and says, "Cheerful picture, you would say?"

"Sure," says Carl. "Apep. Snakes. Darkness. I've got a warm feeling already."

Hassan laughs.

"It looks a thousand years old," Carl continues. "As good a reproduction as I've seen."

Hassan al-Ramin offers a weak smile but no answer. He walks back up the aisle, towards the front of the shop, and picks up a jet-black snake-head mask that is about three times the size of his own cranium. It looks like it might be the oldest object in the building. Hassan turns the snake-face towards his, looks at it for an uncomfortably long moment, then laughs again and sets the mask back on the wooden table where he found it.

The laughter soon fades, though, replaced by a serious tone that slides into Hassan's face like oil sliding across the sea. "I told you not to come here, my friend," he says. "There is nothing for you in this place tonight."

"Salah Aziz," says Kurtzberg.

"What about him?"

"You promised me Salah Aziz. Do you think I came all this way just to visit you night after night?"

Hassan sighs. "I am sorry," he says. 'It will be difficult for you to do business with Salah Aziz. Salah Aziz is not here."

"You promised me that if I waited –"

"*No! No!* I promised you nothing!"

The words are quick, stabbing. They echo around the shop as if fired from a cannon. It is the first time Carl has heard Hassan raise his voice. It will not be the last.

The two men stare at each other for what feels like ten lifetimes before one of them speaks again.

"I promised you nothing," Hassan says again. "Six months ago I tell you that I will take you to Salah when the time is right for you to see him. Since then we have been together twenty-seven times. Twenty-seven times. And I have never lied to you, not once, not ever. I have told you many things, many things that if the wrong person heard me tell you, they would slit my throat without another thought. They would slit my throat! But I have never lied to you. And so why, when I told you that I would take you to see Salah when the time was right, why did you think I was lying then?"

"Hassan, I never said you were lying–"

"I am not sure, my friend," Hassan says, shaking his head. "Because you are here now, even though I asked you not to be. My answers are not enough for you, you do not listen to me about Salah Aziz, and I have to wonder? Why do you follow me to my shop in the middle of the night? Why must you see Salah now? Now, on this night, of all the nights?"

Kurtzberg shrugs, glances towards the store entrance, considers whether he should tell another lie or just keep his mouth shut.

He keeps his mouth shut.

Behind Hassan, in the store windows, Kurtzberg notices shadows shifting on the dirty glass, the silhouettes of children and vagrants, the black ghosts of lost souls lurching in the amber moonlight.

The antique dealer stands there quietly, with his arms folded against his waist.

Kurtzberg sinks back into the row of book shelves. He angles himself toward the red leather-bound book of Apep, his attention once again drawn to the heinous picture of cobra-men engorging themselves on Egyptian soldiers. The hieroglyphics beneath show birds and snakes and wavy lines like water. The symbols mean nothing to the American, but he knows they meant quite something to the person who wrote them so many centuries ago.

"All right, then," says Hassan, finally.

Carl looks up. "All right what?"

"Yes."

"Yes what?"

al-Ramin stands there, blinking. "All right, my friend. Tonight is your lucky night. Let's end this game. I will take you to see Aziz."

Kurtzberg relaxes, but something feels odd. Hassan will take him to Aziz, yes, but if that was always his intention then why pretend at all that Aziz wasn't there?

Before the agent can put voice to his question about Hassan's sudden change of heart, the antiquities dealer walks past him, headed towards the end of the book aisle and around the left corner from there. Motioning for Kurtzberg to follow, he slides a worn rug aside and lifts a bronze ring in the floor that connects with a trap door just wide enough for one man. He motions for Kurtzberg to join him, and a few seconds later they descend into what the agent will later recall as being a certain circle of Hell.

And so the two men walk a darkened corridor underneath Hassan's antique shop. Flickering torches light the way, mounted in the stone every fifteen feet, throwing just enough light to catch the twitchy figures of rats scurrying along the floor's edge. Mold chokes the atmosphere. Considering the part of the world in which he finds himself, Kurtzberg halfway expects a mummy to shuffle by at any moment, dragging its cursed bandages behind.

Maybe twenty yards down, a faint orange glow from the right signals a bend in the corridor and an opening to a large room. Muffled sounds from there suggest human presence: chains dragging, the occasional clank of metal on metal, maybe even muffled voices. What sounds like muffled voices, anyway.

Then – a scream.

A *scream!* Like death approaching, like a demon loosed from the afterworld, like a soul ripped from its moorings.

Hassan moves forward, unfazed, but the wail stops Kurtzberg cold. It pierces the corridor air for five or six seconds that feel like decades to the unnerved agent.

"What... was *that?*"

Hassan turns, makes blank eye contact, but doesn't say a word. He doesn't shrug, he doesn't look surprised, he doesn't look like he cares, he doesn't look like anything. Then he straightens back around and keeps walking.

Soon enough, the scream fades. A few moments after it's gone, another man appears from the room around the bend. He's wearing a dirty white robe and sandals. His head is shaved smooth. He walks towards them, slow, unconcerned that they are there, and he carries a small swaddle in his arms that hides something Kurtzberg can't quite identify at that distance.

As this bald man approaches, the agent's nerves dance. Kurtzberg thinks about the pistol strapped against his chest. But the closer the man gets, the more Carl realizes that the gun won't be necessary right now. This man has no intention of confronting them. He stares straight ahead, into the beyond. Finally he is just a few feet away, and when he brushes numbly past, the agent finally realizes what is inside the swaddle that the approaching man holds in his arms. A small child.

A dead little boy.

A dead little boy?

The agent's pulse skyrockets. *What the hell is going on here?*

He thinks about Tennessee, and his friends on the playground.

His eyes are still adjusting to the flickering light in the tunnel, but now he sees deep scratches in the wall and odd objects lying about: a glass milk bottle, three tennis shoes that can't make one pair, a baby doll head with blonde hair and one eye stuck shut, a rotten blanket flecked by rat shit.

What the hell is going on here?

Kurtzberg hears another scream from down the corridor. Another cry of agony, another scimitar through the antelope's belly.

He looks again at the objects around him – the tiny shoes, the doll head, the blanket – and now he knows. Now he knows. Now he knows. He spins around, thinking he can rush for the ladder that leads back up into Hassan's shop and then get out the door and into his car before anyone catches him, but before he takes even one full step he feels strong hands grab him on both sides.

"Salah Aziz," someone whispers. And again: "Take this one to Salah Aziz."

Muscular fingers clamp down on Kurtzberg's neck. His entire body goes limp, completely against his wishes. One of the assailants reaches inside the agent's shirt, takes the pistol that hangs there and smashes it into a thousand glittering pieces, although Kurtzberg is too concerned for his own safety to consider the amount of strength it must take to turn a .38 caliber handgun into glittering dust.

Moments later, they carry him towards what can only be the place where Salah Aziz waits.

The torch-lit corridor opens up into a large chamber that is five times the size of the antique shop aboveground. Two more bald men in white robes drag Carl across a red carpet that bisects the wide stone floor, running towards what looks like a large bathtub.

They drop him in front of the tub and stand back, but not too far back. Next to him is a smallish Egyptian with a thick black mustache, a man Kurtzberg has never seen before in his life but who appears quite upset about something judging by his gasping Arabic speech. Hassan is nowhere to be found.

Kurtzberg rises to one knee, finding in the bath a young man perhaps thirty years old. He has a narrow but smooth face. His cold green eyes are framed by lashes so long they give the impression of mascara. Carl has no idea what to say but he knows he must say *something.* After a moment he asks simply, "Aziz?" He already knows the answer.

"I am Aziz," confirms the man in the bath, looking away from the Egyptian, who continues pleading just the same.

"My name is Kurtz–"

"You should be on your feet now," says Aziz in a calm voice. "I will finish first with my friend Tariq here, then you."

Kurtzberg hesitates for a moment, feels a knee in his back, stands up the rest of the way. As he rises he sees that Salah Aziz is submerged to his neck, but not in water. In blood. The agent's stomach flips over when a snake – he can't tell which kind, doesn't care which kind – breaks through the surface of the blood, slithering up and around the neck of Aziz, then back down into the red pool.

Tariq – the Egyptian with the thick mustache – never looks at Kurtzberg, despite the interruption. His stare remains fixed on Aziz.

After a moment, Tariq, says, "Please, Salah. I ask for your mercy. I have come here only for my son."

"But your son is not here," says Aziz.

'He is, I know he is, your men brought him here last night –"

"You have been lied to."

Kurtzberg notices more serpents slithering through the bloody bath. An egg eater, a cobra, two horned vipers, a cat snake. He lifts his tongue around in his mouth, searching for the comfort of his own spit, but finds only dry cotton.

Tariq reaches into the back of his waistband. He produces a brown brick, wrapped in plastic. "I bring this back to you," he says, holding it out for Aziz, who says nothing, just smiles. "Take it back. Take it back! Give me my son."

"We had an agreement," says Aziz. "Keep your opium. You love it so."

"No. Take it back."

Aziz shifts position in his bath. He sits more upright, stretches his arms out and grips the edge of the tub with each hand. "I told you. Your son is not here." He shakes his head, slow, shaming. "Your son is not here. No, no. Not here."

"You are a *liar!*" Tariq slams the opium brick into the bath, sending red spray into the face of Aziz.

Salah Aziz lets the blood drip off his face, choosing not to wipe it away. He motions for his two acolytes, and quickly the men come forward and grasp Tariq under the arms. He kicks, and spits, and gnashes at them, fighting to the last thread of his soul, determined that whatever has happened to his son in this chamber will not happen to him now. But he doesn't break free.

Aziz watches the struggle for a full minute, coming forward, towards it. Sensing his next move, the men in white robes relax their grips on Tariq and step away.

When they do, Aziz pounces. He collars Tariq and drags him down into the bathtub, down into the blood, down with the cobras and the egg eaters and the horned vipers and the who-knows-what.

Tariq stops his struggle as soon as face slips beneath the surface. His arms flatten out, limp at his sides, and he holds there until Aziz shoves him back up and away from the tub.

After that, he just stands there, shaking, crying.

Kurtzberg thinks about escape, but he knows that if he takes even one step then Salah's men will run him down.

"Look at this," says Aziz to his men. "The love that a father has for his son. All men should know such love in their lives."

Tariq clasps his hands in front of him, ready to beg.

Aziz purses his lips. "Shhh... shhh. You are not a beggar, my friend. You should be proud of this love." He motions to the shadows over his shoulder. "I have a gift for you."

Tariq looks in the direction to which Azis has pointed, just in time to see a little boy walk out.

His son.

"Farooq!" cries Tariq. "Come to me!" He stoops towards the ground, arms wide, suddenly oblivious to everything around him – Aziz, Kurtzberg, the blood, the snakes, the darkness.

The boy approaches, but as he comes near, Tariq realizes that something is wrong. His son looks cold, faceless, unemotional. He doesn't rush into the chamber with rapturous joy; he just comes to the side of the bathtub and stands, staring at his father with a blank expression that freezes Tariq's heart in his chest.

Aziz reaches for the boy's arm. He pushes him towards Tariq, and the boy edges out the last few steps into the chamber. He wraps his arms around his father's legs but the embrace is limp and meaningless.

Tariq tousles the hair of his child. Tears drip down, cutting through the blood from the bath of Aziz, the blood of men and snakes, the blood which almost drowned Tariq and still paints his skin. He stands there like that for as long as he can, knowing that this is the last time he will ever see his son's face, even if it might not actually be his son here at all.

Then, he lunges forward, at Aziz.

But the blade is too fast..

Tariq hears a sick ka-THUNK, feels the cold rip of steel through his back, then looks down at a gore-darkened piece of honed steel jutting out of his chest. He tastes iron in his mouth as blood geysers from his throat. He collapses at the foot of the tub, rolls over, dying.

And then the snakes come for him.

They slither forward, around Aziz, cascading out of the scarlet bath glistening with an eerie sheen. A huge number of snakes, too many to count, tens, hundreds, maybe thousands, an impossible number teeming forth from the red pool, slick and sliding across the body of Tariq, the Egyptian. Tariq, the opium addict. Tariq, the father, who screams as the reptiles move over him and envelop him in their writhing cascade.

Salah Aziz just watches, unmoved. He flicks his tongue; his irises disappear; his eyes become solid black. With the screams of Tariq still fading into the chamber corners, Aziz once again slips into his pool of blood. But before he disappears, he flashes a terrible smile in the direction of Carl Kurtzberg, and seeing that, Kurtzberg the American agent can think only of the book he saw in Hassan's shop a lifetime ago. The special book on the shelf, the book unencumbered by other books. The book of Apep. The snake. The darkness.

PHILOSOPHER DOG

A comic book
script by Aaron Saylor
story by Aaron Saylor & David Rogers

PHILOSOPHER DOG
Script by Aaron Saylor
Art by David Rogers

Issue #1 - "There's Nothing Wrong with Maybe"

EXT. FIELD - DAY.

A small TERRIER sniffs out a MAN who lies on his
back in a field of green grass. We're very close to
the dog, can't make out much more than his head and
some clothing that is torn in spots.

                    BOX
          Hello?

The dog explores further up the man. Up onto his
chest. There looks like SMOKE rising from the body.

                    BOX
          Hello?

Further up. Neck. Lips. Tufts of smoke coming out
of the mouth.

Further up. The man's eyes are closed.

                    BOX
          Hello?

The dog licks his face. Whimpers.

Wide angle. We see only the terrier's back, as he sits on the man's chest. The animal's head is cocked to one side; he's intrigued. And for the first time we see fully what this is – the dog is sitting on a man lying on his back, his body smoking, his clothes torn.

The man is in his late 20's or early 30's, handsome, but not movie-star handsome, maybe like a grown up Peter Parker. Short hair, neatly trimmed beard. He wears plain clothes - untucked long-sleeve collared shirt, unbuttoned to reveal the plain t-shirt underneath. Blue jeans, black boots, torn and battered though they are.

He's DEAD.

> BOX
>
> Hello?

EXT. CLIFF - NIGHT.   (TWENTY FOUR HOURS AGO)

> RAIDER
>   (box)
>   Hello.

In profile - the silhouetted cliff. In the background, we see the lights of the city, but they're far away, hazy, preceded by an expanse of desert.

On the cliff's edge, we see the silhouette of a DOG, the same small terrier as before - RAIDER. He sits there, looking upward, thinking.

                    RAIDER
                (box)
        It's a nice night, tonight.
        A clear night.

                    RAIDER
                (box)
        A night for questions, and
        answers. Or maybe no answers.
        Maybe just questions. Or,
        maybe just maybes. There's
        nothing wrong with maybes.

The stars.

                    RAIDER
                (box)
        I like to think that it's
        the maybes that lead humanity
        forward.

A nebula, its red and purple gases swirling in the
star field, we're out in deep space now. Comets
swirling among the gases, everything delicately
balanced out in the void.

                    RAIDER
                (box)
        Man wonders: MAYBE we can
        reach the stars. MAYBE there
        is something out there. MAYBE
        we can go further. Maybe, maybe,
        maybe.

                    RAIDER
                (box)
        We are not so different, dogs
        and men. That's one thing I've

                    RAIDER (CONT.)
          learned. Men and dogs, we
          look up at the same stars. We
          ask ourselves the same questions.

                    RAIDER
                   (box)
          WHO am I?

                    RAIDER
                   (box)
          WHAT am I?

                    RAIDER
                   (box)
          What are WE?

Bird's eye-view – a close-up of Raider looking
upward, an expression of deep thought. The stars,
the nebula, reflected in his eyes. This is no
ordinary terrier.

                    RAIDER
                   (box)
          Why are they up there? Why
          are we down here? What lies
          in the stars? What lies BEYOND
          the stars?

                    RAIDER
                   (box)
          So many questions, so few
          answers. And yet for men and
          dogs, these are the thoughts
          that occupy our philosophical
          minds –

                    JOSEPH
               (out of frame)
          Raider! What are you doing out
          here?

Raider looks behind him.

He sees his owner, JOSEPH, a physicist, running
towards him. It's the man we saw in the beginning,
the dead man.

In the background, the ASTRONOMICAL OBSERVATORY
that looms behind Joseph is lit up from the inside.

                    JOSEPH
          I thought we had a deal. No
          more running around at night!

                    RAIDER
               (box)
          That's Joseph.

At Raider now, Joseph scoops the dog into his arms.

                    RAIDER
               (box)
          He works in the lab. He loves
          the stars. He loves me.

                    RAIDER
               (box)
          Joseph is my master, and I'm
          at peace with that. As men go,
          he's a good one.

Smiling, Joseph lifts the dog up above his head.
Looking up at Raider, who hangs in Joseph's hands,
against the starfield now.

The dog almost looks like he's smiling. He's content. His tongue sticks out a little bit.

Terrier's eye view. Joseph walks back to the lab, with Raider right behind.

> JOSEPH
> Come on boy, let's go back to the lab. There's supposed to be a heckuva meteor shower tonight. It'll look great through the telescope. Way better than out here, buddy.

As he runs to keep up, Raider looks straight ahead.

> RAIDER
> (box)
> You got it, buddy.

EXT. OBSERVATORY - NIGHT.

Wide shot of the front of this huge, state-of-the-art building. It cost $500 million dollars to build, and that was a steal. Joseph and Raider standing in front of the large steel-and-glass doors. The sign above the entrance says "FURNACE MOUNTAIN NATIONAL OBSERVATORY."

Joseph punches his security code into the keypad.

INT. OBSERVATORY - NIGHT.

Raider and Joseph walk through a massive lobby, lined on one side by a gigantic sculpture of the SOLAR SYSTEM, on the other side by a long, sleek SECURITY DESK.

The lights are low and dramatic in here, to allow the sculpture's lighting full effect.

Behind the desk is a bank of HI-DEF TELEVISION MONITORS that covers the entire wall. The monitors are all broadcasting what look to be a number of images taken by the Hubble telescope. In front of the monitors, behind the desk, sits a young lady, mid 20s, blonde hair in a pony tail, stylish eyeglasses, cute.

This is LAUREL - she works security at night. What little security is needed. Mostly she reads a lot, which is what she's doing as Joseph and Raider stroll past.

> LAUREL
> What's up, Joseph.

> JOSEPH
> Hey, Laurel.

Raider jumps, barks happily at her.

> LAUREL
> No, I didn't forget you, Raider honey.

She drops a cookie his way.

> LAUREL
> (to Joseph)
> Working late again?

                    JOSEPH
          Sure. Birdy's got a couple
          of guidance sensors that need
          to be replaced. The usual. How
          about you?

Laurel holds up her book - a trashy romance novel.

                    LAUREL
          You know. The usual.

She leans across the desk, smiling, and reaches
down for Raider.

                    LAUREL
          And what about you, little
          guy? You gonna have a big time
          in the lab tonight?

Raider stands on two legs, reaching for hand with
his little paws.

                    RAIDER
                 (box)
          The usual.

                    LAUREL
          You be careful in there, you
          hear me? If the boss found out
          you were running around in here,
          he'd —

                    JOSEPH
          But, of course, he WON'T find
          out.

Now, Joseph leans in on his elbows, halfway across
the desk. Close to Laurel. They're flirting – and
it's clear they've done this before.

                    JOSEPH
          He won't find out, right?

                    LAUREL
          That depends.

                    JOSEPH
          On what?

                    LAUREL
          On how nice the aspiring and
          somewhat attractive young
          physicist is to the girl behind
          the reception desk.

Raider bounds around on his hand legs, excited,
near Joseph's feet.

                    JOSEPH
               (off panel)
          Now, that's interesting. Sounds
          like blackmail to me.

                    LAUREL
               (off panel)
          Sounds like blackmail to me,
          too.

While he's still jumping around, we get Raider's
view from the ground, of Joseph grinning at Laurel,
mischievous.

                    LAUREL
          Hey, you're telling me you
          got something against a little
          blackmail? Since when did you
          get so high and mighty?

                    JOSEPH
          I didn't say that.

                    RAIDER
               (box)
          These two and their little
          games. Winks, and smiles, a
          coy laugh here, a well-placed
          shrug of the shoulders there.
          It's like this every night.

                    RAIDER
               (box)
          Every night.

Joseph takes Laurel's hand, pulls it across the
desk, like he's asking her to dance. We can't see
their faces above their mouths, but there is no
mistaking the warmth between them.

                    JOSEPH
          M'lady, if I might take your
          hand –

                    LAUREL
          Yes, my lord. You may.

                    RAIDER
               (box)
          Gag.

Then they're off! Raider watches Joseph and Laurel, hand in hand, running off into the observatory like two kids on their first big adventure.

The dog is not impressed - he lays down, paws covering his eyes.

> RAIDER
>> (box)
> People.

INT. TELESCOPE ROOM - NIGHT.

Looking down from the ceiling. The massive telescope looms huge in one side of the frame, as Joseph and Laurel come into the room, with Raider trotting in beside them.

> LAUREL
> If your boss knew you
> brought me in here, we'd
> both be out of a job.

> JOSEPH
> I doubt it.

> LAUREL
> Oh, sure. It's just a twenty-
> five BILLION dollar telescope,
> right? Dime a dozen. If anything
> breaks, just call the maintenance
> man and he'll have 'er going again
> in no time.

> JOSEPH
> Actually, it's a THIRTY-FIVE
> billion dollar telescope -

                         LAUREL
           Oh. EXCUSE me.

                         JOSEPH
           - and trust me, for that
           kind of money, you couldn't
           break it with a sledgehammer.

At the base of the telescope, Joseph taps on a
single video monitor attached to the unit. The
base of the telescope itself looks like a
solid, seamless steel cylinder.

NAME
DATE OF BIRTH
SCANNING IRIS...

He bends down, to the glowing screen.

                    COMPUTER VOICE
           Iris confirmed.

A single, tiny joint in the steel HISSES open.
The base slides open, revealing a huge bank of
technology, the best money can buy. Computer
screens showing ASTRONOMICAL ACTIVITY, graphic
analysis, complex data.

Laurel's eyes are wide with amazement.

                    COMPUTER VOICE
           The BRD-40380 is now available
           for full observational use.
           Thank you, Joseph.

                         JOSEPH
           Your welcome, Birdy.

He turns and sees Laurel still amazed, eyes wide, hand over her mouth.

                       JOSEPH
        What's the matter?

                       LAUREL
        I don't usually get to be here
        when it's actually turned on.

Joseph pulls out another touch screen, extending it towards him on a robotic arm.

                       JOSEPH
        Actually, she's ALWAYS on.
        Has to be, if we want her
        to catch everything that's
        happening up there. The
        universe never sleeps, you
        know.

He steps aside from the touch screen and motions her towards it.

                       JOSEPH
        Your turn.

A long shot, from Raider's point of view, across the room. He watches Laurel and Joseph, standing next to each other in front of the telescope's monitors, looking up at the celestial images. The room is a hive of visual information; the two people seem tiny in front of the gigantic machine.

                       LAUREL
        What is that?

                    JOSEPH
          That's a nebula. Looks
          pretty, but not much more
          than a few million stars in
          a dust cloud.

                    LAUREL
          Nice. And that?

                    JOSEPH
          That's Omega Centauri. The
          largest globular cluster in
          the known universe.

                    LAUREL
          Globular cluster. Nice.

                    JOSEPH
          A globular cluster is, uh...
          it's a spherical collection of
          stars that orbits a galactic
          core as a –

She clearly doesn't get it.

                    JOSEPH
          Never mind.

                    RAIDER
               (box)
          I've heard Joseph say more
          than once that if you've seen
          one globular cluster, you've
          seen all. He says it like they're
          as common as pebbles on a beach.

                    RAIDER
             (box)
        Somehow, I don't think he'll tell
        HER that, though.

Laurel, looking up, the starry image reflected from
the monitor onto her face. She looks enthralled.

                    RAIDER
              (box)
        Good move, buddy.

Raider wanders away, through the narrow walk
between the lab wall and edge of the telescope
base. Again, there are monitors everywhere, even
small ones down at Raider's eye level.

                    RAIDER
              (box)
        We spend a lot of time here,
        Joseph and I. It's Joseph's
        job, but sometimes I think it's
        his home, too. The only place he
        really feels comfortable.

                    RAIDER
              (box)
        Nebulae, globular clusters,
        asteroid belts, comets, white
        dwarfs, red dwarfs, dwarfs of
        all colors. I like to think of
        myself as a philosopher, not a
        physicist, and to be honest the
        science runs together for me
        after a while.

                    RAIDER
                (box)
          These days, I don't find much
          to interest me during our
          visits.

Something catches his eye - he turns his head,
looking to the floor-level monitors alongside.

Leans in close.

                    RAIDER
                (box)
          But every now and then...

On the monitor, a STARFIELD. But in one corner of
the screen, a long RIBBON OF LIGHT, some strange
celestial swath.

Closer. The swath seems to be cutting through the
universe... and growing. It's open widest at the
center, with ENERGY spilling out.

                    RAIDER
                (box)
          Every now and then, something
          new comes along...

Closer on the ribbon of light.

Closer... the energy spilling out...

EXT. OUTER SPACE.

The same moment. The Ribbon, for real now. Huge,
hundreds, maybe thousands of miles long, hard to
tell out here in deep space.

Miles above Earth, a manned, American SPACE PROBE
floats in the vacuum. It's narrow, with two large
circular free spinning end pieces connected by a
set of four cylindrical walkways. Rocket boosters
on end of the cylinders. (Go for it – whatever you
want it to look like.) Earth itself can be seen,
but far off in the distance.

We can also make out one lone ASTRONAUT standing on
the outside of the ship, at one far end. He looks
out towards the same RIBBON OF LIGHT that Raider
saw on the telescope.

INT. SPACE PROBE. NIGHT.

A FEMALE ASTRONAUT, young and brainy, hair tied in
a ponytail, headset on, wearing a shirt and slacks.
She HANGS IN ZERO-GRAVITY near her console, legs up
in the air, typing on a keyboard and looking at a
monitor.

                    FEMALE ASTRONAUT
          What is it?

                    ASTRONAUT
               (Off panel)
          I have absolutely no idea. I
          never saw it until the first
          trip out here today.

EXT. SPACE PROBE. NIGHT.

The other astronaut holds on to the tow line that
anchors him to the ship. Now we can see he has a
TOOL KIT strapped to his side.

In the beyond, the light ribbon is noticeably
closer. Bigger.

                    ASTRONAUT
          It's definitely moving. Fast.
          You getting these images back
          to Birdy?

INTERCUTTING - EXT./INT. SPACE PROBE. NIGHT.

                    FEMALE ASTRONAUT
          Absolutely. Doctor Anderson's
          gonna piss himself when he
          sees this.

                    FEMALE ASTRONAUT (CONT.)
          You got any reading on the
          velocity?

                    ASTRONAUT
          None. But it's definitely coming
          this way. We should probably fire
          up those engines and head out a
          few clicks.

                    ASTRONAUT (CONT.)
          You know. Just in case.

                    FEMALE ASTRONAUT
          And we can't do that until you
          get out there and change out
          that exotronic cell. Which is
          why you went out there in the
          first place, remember?

                    ASTRONAUT
          Yeah, your highness. I remember.

EXT. SPACE PROBE. NIGHT.

The astronaut floats off the hull of the probe, into space, anchored by the tether but still several feet off the ship.

                FEMALE ASTRONAUT
            (off panel)
         I keep telling you, I prefer
         "Your Majesty."

                  ASTRONAUT
         Forgive me. Your MAJESTY.

                FEMALE ASTRONAUT
         I'll let this one slide. Just
         get the thing fixed and get
         back in here, okay, babe?

                  ASTRONAUT
         Working on it.

He ends up on the back of the ship, towards the bottom of one of the cylinder ends.

Takes a high-tech REPAIR TOOL out of the bag on his side.

Starts working on the "exotronic cell" (yes, I made that up).

INT. SPACE PROBE. NIGHT.

The female astronaut floats away from the console, checking instrument panels above her.

                    FEMALE ASTRONAUT
          I'll get everything prepped
          in here. Once you finish your
          handiwork outside, we should be
          ready to roll.

                       ASTRONAUT
                    (off panel)
          Perfect.

EXT. SPACE PROBE. NIGHT.

The astronaut pops out the exotronic cell. It's
about the size of his hand.

                       ASTRONAUT
          And the even better news is,
          it looks like a quick fix on
          that damaged cell. Get my seat
          warm for me, will you?

INT. SPACE PROBE. NIGHT.

She's still checking the overhead instruments.
Now a longer shot - as she moves back down towards
the pilots' chairs.

                    FEMALE ASTRONAUT
          Control center, check.

                       ASTRONAUT
                    (off panel)
          Exotronic booster cell, check.

EXT. SPACE PROBE. NIGHT.

Rear view. The astronaut floats back again, away
from the ship.

                    ASTRONAUT
          I'll be down there in five
          minutes. And I'm not kidding
          about the seat. It'd better be
          warm when I get there –

Then he turns to look behind him, and we see
REFLECTED IN HIS FACE SHIELD, THE LIGHT WAVE.

                    ASTRONAUT
             Not good.

Wide reverse angle – the light ribbon is just a few
hundred yards off the edge of the probe. The
astronaut stares straight into it, his arms
helplessly up in front of his face, the light wave
and all its energy about to consume him.

Side angle – the light SLAMS INTO THE PROBE,
ripping up the astronaut and the hull of the ship
all at once!

INT. SPACE PROBE. NIGHT.

Bright light and energy roar through the cabin,
tearing at the female astronaut as she sits in her
pilot's chair, SCREAMING, wracked with pain,
powerless to do anything about it.

EXT. SPACE PROBE. NIGHT.

The energy wave washes across the entire space
probe, and the probe comes apart at the seams in a
massive moment of destruction.

EXT. THE PENTAGON. NIGHT - THREE HOURS LATER.

The center of the United States military looms
large in Washington D.C. A familiar scene to any
American, all lit up at night.

                    SECRETARY
            (from inside the Pentagon)
      I'm sorry, Doctor Anderson,
      but General Isaac is busy at
      the moment -

                 DOCTOR ANDERSON
            (from inside the Pentagon)
      I don't care! I have to get
      in that office!

                    SECRETARY
            (from inside the Pentagon)
      But... he's busy.

                 DOCTOR ANDERSON
            (from inside the Pentagon)
      Didn't you hear me? I DON'T
      CARE IF HE'S BUSY!

INT. PENTAGON. NIGHT.

Physicist DOCTOR ANDERSON - 60's, wild white air,
disheveled clothes, lab coat, very Einstein-like -
BANGS on a closed office door, with one hand. In
the other hand, he holds PICTURES of the ENERGY
WAVE, as sent by the space probe. The SECRETARY is
trying to pull him back.

There's been some excitement. The secretary looks
wracked with frustration. The doctor is clearly in
a hurry.

He continues hammering on the door with his fist, not even turning around to acknowledge the secretary.

                    SECRETARY
          Sir, if you would like to
          schedule an appointment for
          later in the month –

                    DOCTOR ANDERSON
          Oh, I'd like to schedule an
          appointment, all right. For
          right now.

The scientist turns around to face her.

                    SECRETARY
          I'm sure General Isaac would
          be happy to talk, at a time
          that might be more convenient
          for both of you–

                    DOCTOR ANDERSON
          Great. You know what would be
          a really convenient time for
          both of us? How about RIGHT NOW?

                    DOCTOR ANDERSON (CONT.)
          I'm pretty sure right now would
          work for me.

A close-up. The door cracked open, a bit of the general's face exposed. He squints, looks out, pissed.

The door opens. GENERAL ISAAC stands there, tall, broad, rock-jawed, powerful, in his early 50's. Looming in the doorway, behind the physicist.

                         GENERAL ISAAC
                 Fine, Anderson. Now will work.

The secretary looks frantic.

                          SECRETARY
                 I'm sorry, General, I tried to
                 keep him out —

                       DOCTOR ANDERSON
                 Your secretary was very helpful.
                 She did her best to stop us from
                 saving the planet.

The secretary rolls her eyes.

Anderson snubs her.

                       DOCTOR ANDERSON
                 Go ahead. Roll your eyes.

He turns back to the general.

                       DOCTOR ANDERSON
                 We have to act. There isn't
                 much time —

General Isaac just walks back into his office.

                         GENERAL ISAAC
                 Much time for what?

Anderson runs after him.

INT. GENERAL ISAAC'S OFFICE.

Isaac sits at his desk now. Doctor Anderson slams
both hands on the desk, looking desperate.

                    DOCTOR ANDERSON
         We have a situation here,
         General, and I can't stress
         enough how dire this could be –

He holds one of the energy-wave photos out for the
general, who looks at it, unimpressed.

                    GENERAL ISAAC
         Riiiiight. Clearly. A situation.

The doctor throws up his hands, exasperated, walks
away.

                    DOCTOR ANDERSON
                 (to himself)
         Again, the brilliant minds of
         the military choose to ignore
         the obvious reality in front
         of their own faces.

He spins back to the general, frantically waving
the pictures in front of him.

                    DOCTOR ANDERSON
         I don't think you understand.
         These images were taken by the
         BRD-40380's celestial probe just
         a couple of hours ago. If they're
         any indication of what we can
         expect –

                    GENERAL ISAAC
         The BRD... 4...0...3... what?

                    DOCTOR ANDERSON
          The Birdy. The largest space
          observation project in the
          history of humankind, funded
          by your government and mine to
          the tune of a couple TRILLION
          dollars.

General Isaac clearly doesn't get it.

                    DOCTOR ANDERSON
          That neat little toy that also
          helps you drop guided missiles
          into cave openings the size of a
          refrigerator.

                    GENERAL ISAAC
          Oh. That.

Anderson looks down, holding his forehead,
irritated.

He grabs Isaac by the arm, pulling him up, much to
the general's surprise.

                    DOCTOR ANDERSON
          Come here.

                    GENERAL ISAAC
          Hold on, Anderson –

At the window, Anderson stands by the window,
pointing up to the sky.

Reverse angle – he's pointing up at the ENERGY
WAVE, which is bigger in the sky now. The general
looks up at it, too.

                    DOCTOR ANDERSON
          THERE is your situation.

They walk back away from the window.

                     GENERAL ISAAC
          I'm afraid you're gonna have
          to give me a little more than
          THAT, doctor.

Anderson talks over his shoulder as he walks back
to Isaac's desk.

                    DOCTOR ANDERSON
          It's some sort of energy wave.
          The truth is, we don't know much
          about it at this point. It wasn't
          showing on any charts until a
          couple of days ago, when our
          astronauts on the space probe
          noticed some high gamma activity
          in the EM spectrum a couple
          million miles towards Mars.

The doctor moves to sit in the general's chair.

                     GENERAL ISAAC
                    (off panel)
          What do these astronauts of
          yours have to say now?

                    DOCTOR ANDERSON
          Nothing.

He leans back in the chair, looking at the ceiling.

                    DOCTOR ANDERSON
          We lost them when the energy
          wave passed over.

General Isaac stands in front of his desk now,
looking at Anderson.

                    GENERAL ISAAC
          So, this energy wave... what
          kind of threat does it pose
          to us?

                    DOCTOR ANDERSON
          On a scale of 1 to 10?

They stare at each other.

                    DOCTOR ANDERSON
          I'd say a fifteen.

EXT. LAUREL'S HOUSE. NIGHT.

A little house, out in the suburbs. Neatly trimmed
lawn, trees, clean.

INT. LAUREL'S APARTMENT. NIGHT.

Joseph and Laurel sit on the couch, in the
background. There's is a LAPTOP COMPUTER open on
the coffee table in front of them. In the
foreground, Raider sits on his hind legs, looking
at another YORKSHIRE TERRIER who bounces around
like a maniac, with her tongue hanging out.

                    RAIDER
                  (box)
          This one's a genius.

He lays down, covering his eyes.

                     RAIDER
            (box)
     Make it stop, please.

The other dog moves in, sniffing Raider.
He turns away, looking at Joseph with a forlorn
look that plainly says, "Get me out of here."

Joseph gets up off the couch.

                     JOSEPH
     All right, Raider. I hear
     you.

                     LAUREL
     Come on. Let them play. They'll
     be fine. I think Gracie likes
     him.

Gracie looks overjoyed at her ability to run in
circles. Raider looks unenthused.

Joseph picks up Raider, dangles him in the air,
smiling at him.

                     JOSEPH
     Nah, he looks like he's
     getting bored. Aren't you,
     buddy?

Raider sticks his tongue out, playing and looking
dumb for Laurel's benefit.

                     RAIDER
            (box)
     Not exactly, buddy.

                    RAIDER
              (box)
         "Getting bored" would imply
         that I was entertained in the
         first place.

A MESSAGE BOX comes up on the LAPTOP SCREEN. It
says, "INCOMING VIDEO MESSAGE". Behind the laptop,
across the room, we can see Joseph putting Raider
back down.

                    LAUREL
              (off panel)
         Looks like you've got a
         caller.

Joseph plays with Raider, while the other terrier
dances among them.

                    JOSEPH
         Who is it?

Laurel spins the laptop around so he can see it. On
the screen, DOCTOR ANDERSON.

                 DOCTOR ANDERSON
              (from laptop screen)
         Joseph, I'm afraid I have
         some bad news.

Joseph grabs one corner of the monitor.

Looks at it. Intent.

Then, his eyes show some concern.

Raider looks as though he senses something might be
going on.

The dog walks over to where Joseph stood near the laptop.

From Raider's POV - Only now, Joseph is holding his arm out, telling Laurel -

> JOSEPH
>
> Wait here.

> LAUREL
>
> What's going on?

> JOSEPH
>
> I'll be right back.

He turns, in a hurry.

On the screen - Doctor Anderson looks scared to death.

Raider watches Joseph throw the door open and run out in one motion.

> RAIDER
>
> YELP!

> RAIDER
>   (box)
> Huh. That was interesting.
> I haven't seen Joseph react
> like that since he hit level
> 50 on World of Warcraft.

Takes off after his master.

> RAIDER
>   (box)
> Hold on!

Gracie runs after both of them.

Raider jumps for the open door.

> RAIDER
> (box)
> I'll be right there!

Gracie catches him. Tackles him.

> RAIDER
> (box)
> Great. Something's definitely
> up with Joseph, but instead
> of finding out what I have to
> deal with the genius again.

Reverse angle - Joseph's face, looking into the sky
with a mixture of amazement and stark terror.
Behind him, we can see Gracie and Raider rolling
around on the ground playfully.

They roll up behind him.

Raider gets the upper hand on Gracie and strides
above her, looking up at Joseph.

> RAIDER
> (box)
> Joseph?

Laurel appears in the doorway.

> LAUREL
> Joseph, what's wrong —

                    LAUREL (CONT.)
          (to herself)
      Ohmigosh.

A stunning vista - Joseph standing on the lawn,
with Raider and Gracie at his feet, and all of them
looking up at the sky, at the ENERGY WAVE that
looms almost as large as the sky itself. Trees
whipping around. Lightning. Dust billowing on the
ground.

Joseph whips his head around -

                    JOSEPH
          LAUREL! GET OUT -

Too late.

The energy wave slams into the earth. Joseph,
Raider, Gracie, the house, all take the brunt.

The neighborhood.

The city.

The western US.

The entire Earth.

Flames, light, disintegration.

And then, nothing. Black.

Black.

                    BOX
          Hello?

EXT. FIELD - DAY.

Back to where we started the story. A small
TERRIER, sniffing out JOSEPH, who lies on his back
in a field of green grass. We're very close to the
dog, can't make out much more than his head and
some clothing that is torn in spots.

Only it's not a he. It's not Raider - it's GRACIE.

                    BOX
          Hello?

The dog explores further up the man. Up onto his
chest. There looks like SMOKE rising from the body.

                    BOX
          Hello?

Further up. Neck. Lips. Tufts of smoke coming out
of the man's mouth.

Further up. Joseph's eyes are closed.

                    BOX
          Hello?

The dog licks his face. Whimpers.

Wide angle. We see only the terrier's back, as she
sits on the man's chest. The animal's head is
cocked to one side; she's intrigued. And for the
first time we see fully what this is - Joseph,
lying on his back, his body smoking, his clothes
torn.

He's DEAD.

He's not dead.

His eyes open, barely.

                    RAIDER
              (off panel)
         Hello?

Joseph rolls over, barely lifting his head, but
enough to see...

A blurry image of what looks like THE SPACE PROBE,
on the ground.

The blurry image clarifies – it's definitely the
probe lying several yards away, perfectly intact!
And the two astronauts sitting on top of it,
looking at him!

Joseph wipes his eyes. Just can't believe it.

                   JOSEPH
        What the –

                    RAIDER
              (off panel)
        Joseph! Turn around!

Joseph rolls over, head laying back in the grass.
Again, he raises up, looking now in the opposite
direction from the space probe. And the look on his
face says one thing: HOLY CRAP.

Reverse angle – and now we see the whole picture,
an amazing sight beneath a bright sky filled with
wispy clouds. Joseph is looking at Gracie bouncing
maniacally, tail wagging, full excitement. And next
to her is RAIDER.

Only it's not just Raider, it's a slightly larger version of RAIDER. STANDING ON TWO LEGS. Holding a small GREEK XIPHOS SWORD. Dressed in full GREEK ARMOR. And behind Raider, a very large and very angry GREEK ARMY, hundreds of armored men and horses, looking like they are out for blood.

                    RAIDER
          We might have a problem here.

                    THE END

ABOUT THE AUTHORS

AARON SAYLOR lives up around Louisville way with his wife, Leslie and their philosopher dog Lily. He loves the smell of fresh-cut grass and tries to watch at least one movie a day. Let him know if you've got a poker game going.

STROTHER KEVIN HALL is a native of Powell County, Kentucky, a University of Kentucky graduate and a current resident of Georgetown. He has several incomplete projects floating around and thinks it's about time to start knocking them out again.

www.ingramcontent.com/pod-product-compliance
Lightning Source LLC
Chambersburg PA
CBHW060421130626
46555CB00005B/2158